EX LIBRIS

ANNE BARRY

THURSDAY'S CHILD

RUTH KIRKLEY

MINERVA PRESS
MONTREUX LONDON WASHINGTON

THURSDAY'S CHILD

Copyright © 1995 Ruth Kirkley

ISBN 1 85863 264 1

First Published 1995 by
MINERVA PRESS
10 Cromwell Place
London SW7 2JN

Printed in Great Britain by
Martins the Printers Ltd., Berwick upon Tweed

THURSDAY'S CHILD

CONTENTS

CHAPTER ONE

LOOK LOWER THAN AN ANGEL WING

I'd looked forward to going to school as I realized that often I was bored at home. There were so many restrictions: "Where've you put the scissors?" "Come and help me dry the dishes." "Tidy your drawer." "Tidy your things off the table." "Set the table." "Clear the table." "Pop down to the shop to get half a pound of tomatoes." Stop doing this, that and the other. The house had always to be tidy and so did everyone in it. This was no problem as far as clothes went, as once dressed I stayed in the same things all day and was fairly clean, but my hair too had to be tidy. This wasn't easy when you have a large bow on one side which is too tight to start with and too slack after half an hour.

My mother's hair was fine and tended to fly away so she worked hard at mine. She would have liked to have each individual hair permanently fixed and it was a pity we lived before the days of hair spray. We both wore hats of course, mine was a knitted pixie hood with a pom-pom while Mam had a black trilby type hat with trailing draperies down the back. It was very dramatic and I liked her in it and had no patience with her worries that people might think her a widow. Later, during the war there was a poster of a gaunt tragic woman in black headed KEEP DEATH OFF THE ROADS and at that point my mother regretfully laid her hat to rest. People did think her a widow and I came in for some unnecessary sympathy but that didn't trouble me. Dad was out so much that I only saw him at weekends so it amounted to the same thing.

The weekends were taken up with going to the library and to church and to Sunday School and, delight upon delight, going to the fish and chip shop. I preferred going out because there wasn't much to do inside the house. We only possessed one pair of scissors and they were used for food and hair and nails and string and any cutting out job anyone had. We spent more time looking for them than using them and they were never very sharp.

Sometimes I had a ball and could play in the street, sometimes a top and whip and sometimes a hoop. Well, the hoop was usually someone's whose Father kept interesting things in his garage; but I did have a tricycle that I was very proud of. It was useful to barter a ride for a turn with a hoop. I don't think I can have been much use as an entrepreneur as my voice expressed apology rather than conviction in negotiations; the fact that I often had to go looking for my trike when my customer had abandoned it, indicates that no-one thought I had had the best of the bargain.

All children were turned out to play every day unless it was pouring and this was fine if others were there too. Some disappeared for ever when they went to school, barely managing to say "Hello" in the street when actually brought face to face with you. As a non-initiate, I became inarticulate in front of one-time friends and early learned the politics of hierarchy and ageism. When asked if they liked school, their eyes sought the middle distance and their "yes" was breathed out with the solemnity of an oath taker. I thought this represented unspeakable marvels and later, when asked by even younger ones, disguised my own disillusion by similar intimations of wonder.

The thought of going to school was exciting and I only began to get nervous a day or two before the great day. School was certainly not as marvellous as I'd been led to believe. I had a teacher who was mad about handkerchiefs. Every day we had to show one - a clean one - and woe betide the child who couldn't produce one. It was no excuse to say you didn't have a cold so didn't need one, you still were called out to stand in disgrace in the walk-in cupboard.

Even at school there was an awful lot of tidying this up and putting that away and being careful of such and such. The greatest disgrace was to wet the floor and we all echoed the teacher's horror when there was a pool under someone's chair.

Until, of course, a pool was noticed under my own chair and so I learned that there but for the grace of God go I.

Learning to read seemed to take ages and the series of Beacon Books interminable. The only thing that kept me going was a character called Ruth, my own name, who appeared in some of them. Whether those awful Turkey-Lurkey and Chicken-Licken were in the same books I neither know nor care, but at this stage can sympathise with the teacher.

My mother had always read to me so I had no need to be convinced of the value of the written word. The only problem was

when we disagreed about what to read. I liked Alice in Wonderland
- well all the bits except the Caterpillar with the hookah - but my
mother didn't like it at all. She would read short passages to me,
but never took a good long run at it, so I had to weigh up whether I
wanted a long story or one I really liked.

We had books in the house of course but they seemed to be either
on religion or poetry. My favourite book was the News Chronicle
Dictionary which had some splendid illustrations in it. There was a
whole page illustrating a range of fish with pale blue water near the
top ranging down to indigo at the foot. The fish got flatter as you
went down, with the exception of a brilliant blue electric eel, which
was my favourite and to which I turned frequently for the frisson of
horror it gave me. Later, I was to appreciate this book for a more
practical reason: it held a list of words in regular use for
crosswords. It was a good job it had something so useful as it
seemed to be an expurgated dictionary and fell out of favour when I
became adolescent.

As soon as I could read properly I was allowed to get Sunny
Stories every week. The delights of Saturday multiplied. I don't
think I got my whole moral teaching from Sunny Stories, as I went
to church twice a week from the age of four, but I got a great deal.
There was a weekly story about the animals who lived in a huge tree
called the Magic Far-Away Tree.

This was enormously tall and easy to climb and had a slide down
the centre for when you wanted to leave. All sorts of naughty
children climbed that tree to be taught terrible lessons by the saintly
squirrels and bears and owls or whatever. It was always clear what
the naughty behaviour was and sadly, the time came when I was able
to anticipate the punishment so the spice went out of the story. But
the sense of justice I eventually acquired probably came more from
Enid Blyton than Moses.

I suppose I developed a sense of justice at the same time as most
children. I could wail "It's not fair" with the best. It wasn't fair
that I had to go to bed so early, that I could only have one library
book a week, that we couldn't play out on Sunday. The criteria was
what other families did that I wanted to do, not what they had that I
didn't. The property lesson was learned early in the Baker's shop.
Mam took me in and asked me, as she usually did, what cake I
would like for my tea. This time I varied from the usual and chose

an angel wing. Long had I lusted after this piece of puff pastry with cream. The angel cost a penny ha'penny while my usual cake cost only a penny so my mother told me to choose again. I knew there was another customer waiting behind me so, hoping this would create a form of pressure on Mam, I again said I wanted the angel wing. There now ensued a battle between us that rocked the shop. So vehement was I that the other customer joined in and Mam had to explain that she couldn't afford the extra ha'penny. The lady then offered to pay the extra herself. This really put the fat in the fire and I knew that the angel wing was gone for ever. The cheaper cake was bought for me and we went home to a tearful session in which I learned never, never to accept charity and indeed, never to allow myself to get into a position where charity was necessary. The lesson was so well learned that I can still picture the shop and the lady and the neutral girl behind the counter and what my mother was wearing. For many years I found it difficult to accept any offer.

Once David, my new brother arrived, the visits to the Bakery were purely for bread and the only cakes we ever had were home-made ones on Sundays. I eventually had an angel wing many years later and found for myself what a poor thing it was.

Just how deep the lesson had gone no-one knew, least of all my mother, until I went for my inoculation against diphtheria. After a long walk to the church hall and an even longer wait in a crowded, overheated waiting area I went through to be done, being as brave as anyone else. When it was finished the doctor offered me a sweet from a green dish. Although I would have loved the sweet I declined. The doctor saw that I had been taught to say " No" when I meant "Yes" so offered again. When I said "No" the second time my mother said it was all right to take it. "No Thank You." Another battle ensued as this time my mother tried to persuade me that the sweet was really like medicine but I was adamant and told the doctor that I did like sweets, but I didn't have any to offer in return so couldn't accept his.

Not only did I win a moral victory over greed and an educational victory over my mother, but I won an emotional victory that was to ensure no further discussion on the whole topic of accepting gifts. This also happened in a Bakery. We had gone from the church hall to buy bread and while there I fainted. No doubt the walk in cold air, the wait in hot air, the inoculation, the cold air outside then the hot bakery induced the faint, but as a tactical move in this particular engagement it was conclusive.

Actually, I wasn't a particularly aggressive girl: in fact the reverse, as I was encouraged to be quiet in company. That is, after the age of two. When I was two I bit a girl who lived along the street from me. There was no malice in me towards her and it can't have been a very deep bite as the skin wasn't broken. But the teeth marks were clear and I wasn't sorry. My mother, when called, wouldn't believe it had been me but even then I was sensible enough to keep quiet although I certainly understood that biting was unacceptable.

In the Beginners Department at Sunday School I was chosen to be Mary in a Nativity Play, so presumably I looked fairly long suffering. The role was not stressful as I had no dialogue and just had to sit on a large chair with Jesus on my knee. Joseph sat on a similar chair and took no notice of me. The teachers must have had modern ideas about participation as they chose a boy as Jesus, not a doll. Not only was he the same size as me, indeed, he may have been slightly larger, but he knew that he was the star of the show. He absolutely refused to sit on my knee. He refused to sit beside me on the chair. He refused to sit on Joseph's knee and you would think that male solidarity would have been acceptable. He eventually had a chair to himself while Joseph and I squeezed into the other. The teachers seemed unable to establish the traditional triumvirate so there was talk of us wearing labels to tell the audience who was who. In fact, the play was not shown to anyone and my parents were disappointed. I had sat silent and biddible through all this and quite enjoyed the disgrace of the Jesus boy. To crown it all, my parents knew his parents and that made his disgrace worse and my apathy praiseworthy.

I had certainly learned to keep my own counsel. The obligation to answer every question and respond to every overture, is a burden that comes after the age of about four. We had recently moved to a new house and the builder was on site overseeing work further up the street. The road ended outside our house so he parked his car just by our door. One day when I had finished dinner and been excused, I took a brushload of white paint from some handy tin and painted the side of his car. It had looked easy but I was disappointed to find painting was harder than it looked so didn't do as much as I'd planned. I returned to the dinner table. A short while later the builder came rampaging in, accusing me of ruining his car. My parents were amazed and able to show me sitting at the dinner table while I was quite unperturbed. I looked at him in wide-eyed silence. My parents never knew that I had done it though the builder was, I am sure, unconvinced. I had a mild interest in seeing the car in the next few days with dull smudges to indicate where I had been busy.

It took a few more years to teach me to feel guilty.

I grew up in a society of women. My father was out all day and all evening with his work and church and Masons, and at weekends he was at church several times on Sunday. One grandfather was dead, while the other went to the pub occasionally and never spoke to me. Going to the pub was considered much the same as an excursion to hell, so perhaps this affected my conversational expectations. He rarely spoke to my mother either so she found it difficult to encourage anything more than the basic civilities. My mother's brother, Uncle Bill, travelled away from home a lot and was going through something upsetting called a divorce so mustn't be pestered. My father had four sisters, but no brothers and none of these aunties ever managed to escape from their mother into marriage. The only other man in the family was Uncle Alf and he lived in London. When he did visit, the house was transformed. There was laughter and visits to theatres and half crowns slipped into my hand. He was actually interested in what I had been doing and learning and told me jokes about Mickey Mouse that he must have saved up for me.

Even then, aged perhaps four or five, I asked why the jokes were always about Mickey or Donald or Pluto. Were there no girl cartoon characters? Obligingly, he switched to Minnie Mouse and I was mollified for some time until I realized that I had only once seen a cartoon with Minnie in and even then she was just a nagging stay-at-home and Mickey had all the action.

The teachers at school and at Sunday School were all women and the people you met and talked to in the street were all women too. The shop assistants were women, even those who came round to the house to take down your grocery order each week. There were other people's fathers, but they never recognised you when you were in the street alone. So I knew few men and had no examples of happy married life around me. My parents certainly considered themselves happily married, but their times together were late in the evening, when I was safely in bed.

There were happy times playing on the field at the top of the street. There were lots of butterflies and flowers and rhubarb in season to pick from the farmer's field where we weren't supposed to go. Sadly, The News Chronicle Dictionary had no illustrated page of butterflies and as city children we didn't know the names of anything. We had a rope on a tree and took turns swinging out over a small drop. After my return from evacuation I was able to identify several birds and plants and we also had a den from which we kept a lookout for German spies. By then I was quite big and spent a long time after tea doing hand stands against a wall or trying to walk upside down like a crab. But that was maturity.

The streets and the local shops and the field became my known and absolutely safe world. Far more interesting than school. Nesbits was where I had demanded the angel wing, but the girls who served never stayed long. Two large loaves was a regular order and I remember the pleasure when a new law said that bread must be wrapped. Supplies of tissue paper had been provided and the sheets had been precision cut to the size of the loaf. If you bought one loaf there was about half an inch spare to wrap over, but the same size paper was used for two loaves so it didn't quite meet and you were handed a bundle to put into your shopping bag which you could neither hold with one hand nor keep the paper on. This was considered the fault of the Government for making unnecessary rules or yourself for being clumsy, never the size of the paper. The new regulation provided an even greater health hazard as the salesgirl licked her thumb each time she took a fresh piece of paper.

I liked going into Nesbits as it was warm and clean and had a Post Office at one end. This was never busy and you rarely saw anything going on except purchases of stamps and postal orders. I had a proprietorial attitude to Post Offices as my eldest aunt had the Post Office in St Anthony's. This was only about four miles away in distance, but a world away in attitudes. The Post Office there was constantly packed out with people who spent a fortune on postal orders for the pools or got pensions for this that or the other. Aunty Hope despised them all and thought them all scroungers. She was to stay in charge till she retired at sixty-five and I don't think the idea of service or liking her customers ever crossed her mind. She never told a joke or repeated an anecdote and was too mean to engage anyone to help her with the very considerable workload, except a younger sister to whom she paid a pittance. Overwork no doubt added to her disapproval of people in general and her niece in particular.

Next to Nesbits was Robsons the Greengrocer. Mrs Robson herself presided over the potatoes and basic vegetables. Nothing much beyond the peas, beans, carrots, swede, sprouts and cabbage. Salad items were only there in the summer. The shop was dark and dirty and smelt of soil and bare floorboards. I wasn't allowed to pass comments as Mrs Robson might take offence and this seemed to matter since her family owned it. The other side of the shop was a sweet shop and Mrs Robson came round the counter to serve me my Spanish liquorice, gob stopper, sherbet or, if I had more than the usual penny, two ounces of black bullets.

A short distance away was the Stores. This was the Co-op and a very important part of northern life. Nearly every family was a member and took a proportionate share in the profits. The small receipts were marked with your family number and totalled quarterly. The more you spent, the more you got back in dividend. This was one of the few ways women could get a small amount of money together for themselves, and it was the foundation of my mother's quite sizeable nest egg. If you left your dividend in, you could use it as security for a loan to buy some big item in the large store in the centre of town. That was how we bought all our household things and sometimes shoes. There was a price to pay in that some people looked down on those of us who used the Stores.

I liked shopping at the Stores if it wasn't too busy. It was like four shops in one and even a small amount of shopping took quite a time. Butter was a huge mound just as it came out of the barrel, while sugar was in a great tub on the floor. Butter and cheese had to be cut to your requirements and woe betide the customer who objected to a higher price because the assistant wasn't a good judge of quantity. The sugar was measured into home-made sugar paper bags and you had to take care how you handled it else it streamed out into your shopping bag. Shopping took ages with all this going on and the assistants walked back and forth fetching and carrying what you wanted. No time for ditherers.

Shops didn't seem very conveniently placed and no-one seemed to notice opportunities. For example, there was no cobbler, newsagent, no haberdashery close by and the demarcation lines seemed strictly drawn. Shopkeepers certainly felt they were doing the customers a favour just by being there.

My mother felt this most acutely. She had little self-confidence to start with and the offhand patronage undermined her self-esteem further. Most of her generation had had to give up work on marriage and this was a form of cruelty she tolerated without recognising. She loathed housework and had no spare cash to get out of the house much. Dad was never around until late at night and she was bored out of her mind. She even felt it was her fault that she was discontented, so hadn't the confidence to articulate her frustration. She did look lovely in her widow's hat, but I wonder what subconscious feelings dictated the choice.

Much of our small amount of social life was at Church and I liked Sunday School and Anniversaries and annual outings. I also liked singing hymns. Mam didn't really care for any of the services and resented the time Dad spent there. She didn't say she didn't believe half of what she heard, as that would have hurt him but she made it clear that she hated Sundays. In fact, she lived vicariously through my brother and myself. She learned about everyone in our classes and encouraged us both in total recall. Whenever a newcomer joined, her first question to me was "What does her father do?" Quite early on I became embarrassed at her contempt for certain occupations, but it took years to realize what an unacceptable question it was. She had absorbed the class hierarchy thoroughly and seeing us as middle class, though on the bottom rung, she jealously preserved distinctions between those marginally lower. Her salvation came later when we were both at Secondary School and she felt able to take a part-time job.

Life was full of routine with washing day and rice pudding every Monday, a visit to Grandma every Friday, chips from the chip shop every Saturday and weekly doses of syrup of figs to keep us regular. Friday was also hair-washing and bath night and Mam complained that she had too much to do. However, she loved washing my hair and used Green kitchen soap to wash it then put some vinegar in the water to rinse it. Despite this harsh treatment, I had the sort of dark wavy hair she wished she had, so I always had to keep it tidy.

Small shops, small distances, small events in the life of a small girl. But safe. Protected from crime, hurtful remarks, and too much failure. There were certainties of behaviour and position and right and wrong even if the horizons were fairly narrow. Mam's in the kitchen, God's in his heaven and all's right with the world.

Even the coming war was something which would be coped with.

CHAPTER TWO

PULLING UP BLUEBELLS BY THE ROOTS

Everything seemed calm and normal before I was evacuated to Tebay, a tiny village in Cumbria, yet amazingly everything seemed calm and normal once I had settled down in the village pub. And coming from a teetotal family that took some coming to terms with. The demon drink, who had blighted my great grandfather's life before he got religion, causing him to sell a working shipyard for a hundred pounds, lurked in the long stone corridors and actually lived in the bar. In the two years I was there I never entered the bar itself; it was the centre of badness and a horrible smell hung about it permanently, although I did eventually go into the Top room, the Tap room and the Snug. I was so disappointed with the Snug. It was the reverse of cosy and there was the demon smell there too. But with great self denial, or at least being too nervous to object, my parents had agreed to my staying at a public house.

Mam and Dad might not like the alcoholic surroundings and they might suspect unscrupulous people of trying to make me addicted to drink, but they did appreciate Mr Thorn and Auntie's willingness to take any child sent to them. About fifty of us children, in the last stages of exhaustion, had been brought to the Methodist Church hall and put on display. Those who were to take the children arrived to select the one they fancied, but Auntie was too fat to walk so far and had said she would take any girl sent to her. It had to be a girl as Thelma was already there and we would have to share a bed. The gentleman who took me to the Cross Keys offered to hold my hand, but I declined having been taught to distrust men making seemingly kind offers.

Everyone knew I had come from Newcastle with the others from my school, so the conversation turned on how old I was. I told them I was six and this was followed by amazement and the need to know when my birthday was. Then came questions about how my parents could spare me. This was harder as the truth was I had been determined to be evacuated, and had pestered my parents until I had undermined their confidence, and they convinced themselves it was

God's will. The actual arrival at The Cross Keys was rather an anti-climax. I was too tired to respond more than curtly to inquiries about my age, my birthday and whether my parents would miss me, so with great thankfulness I was put to bed.

And so began two years in a totally different world. I don't know if God did have it all planned for me, but I do know all those kind people, whom I have never seen since, played a creative part in my development.

I didn't think they were kind at the time. Mr Thorn never said an unkind word to me, but I had been warned about him. The story told by Thelma and not denied by Auntie, was that he had been drunk one night and chased them round the kitchen with a red hot poker. I never saw him drunk in the years I lived with them, but I always glanced up whenever he came into the kitchen to see what condition he was in. His reputation hinted of danger. I even inquired if it was the same poker and looked at that with fresh eyes. Mr Thorn worked long hours in the Cross Keys for seven days every week and never took a holiday and was also much in demand as a dry stone-waller. He had to be reminded again and again to do the repair, and the gap he eventually tackled was far greater than the original one, but apparently he was worth waiting for. He was also the village photographer and had a well equipped dark room where the cold water tap sometimes ran for twenty-four hours at a stretch. Although this worried me dreadfully as it might help the Enemy, and certainly cause "Want" in later life, I was thrilled to watch the Bride and Groom appear clear and sharp and smiling from blank paper at the bottom of the bath. Even Mr Thorn seemed relieved to have the prints ready a week or two before the couple's baby was born and to have finished with the whole village pestering him.

Auntie had lost heart at having to nag to get anything done, so had given up wearing corsets and dressed always in a large pinny. She had also given up the marital bed and squeezed herself into Auntie Betty's single one. She felt totally unappreciated even by the two evacuees, so had appropriated our butter ration and to this day I can tell the difference between butter and margarine. I didn't mind Auntie having my butter but I did begrudge Auntie Betty having any. After all, she didn't scrub miles of corridor before breakfast, clean the bar and the snug and the tap room, do all the cooking and cleaning of bedrooms, wash and iron and keep an active eye on two young girls.

I only saw Auntie glow once. That was when Wilf came home on leave for a short spell and she squeezed into a dress and laughed and joked.

Auntie Betty was supposed to be in charge of Thelma and me and indeed, for several weeks she did take me to the bathroom on Fridays and supervise my bath. As the weather got colder however, she stayed by the fire and gave instructions and when the frost was sparkling on the insides of the windows I wasn't even sent up. I always washed, Auntie saw to that, but it was just the visible bits and she never knew that my middle was never even dampened and that dirt was engrained between my toes.

Auntie Betty embroidered. She embroidered all morning, all afternoon and most evenings. How she managed to avoid being called up I do not know. There must have been a tame doctor in the village, as there were several girls of the same age, although they certainly didn't sit around all day. She embroidered tablecloths, tray cloths, trolley cloths, napkins, dressing table mats, dressing table runners, table runners, and every other imaginable piece of linen for her bottom drawer. For herein lay Auntie Betty's claim to distinction. She was engaged to be married. She must have had enough linen to start a hotel - which turned out to be somewhat over optimistic as her fiancé was a cobbler and though comfortable, in somewhat more modest circumstances. At least her bottom drawer would last a lifetime. But I wonder if she carried on after marriage? I had never seen her do anything else and the thought of her ever mounting pile of household linen, all to be washed and ironed, is quite frightening.

And all Auntie Betty's embroidery was Lazy Daisy stitch!

Children accept many things uncritically because they have no standards of comparison, but evacuees did have standards of comparison. My new life was as serene as my previous life although I knew I was tolerated and accepted rather than loved. I never for one moment doubted that my parents loved me and that I was special to them. That gave me the confidence to keep one or two different values from the family which now enfolded me.

The values were different not conflicting. There were three dogs, a cat, a tortoise and a parrot chained to a bar which occasionally shouted "Little brown jug I love thee", but no books that I can remember. The parrot was old. Who could imagine that such a colourful bird was over sixty and had been on that bar for much of his life. I couldn't cope with that idea, so I decided that I didn't like him and avoided the whole corner of the kitchen behind the chair Auntie occasionally sat down in. I didn't mind the youngest dog who was called Dot and showed me some affection, but when I was pressed to say which was my favourite animal, I always plumped for the tortoise. The tortoise was no trouble and even hibernated for several months a year which was convenient. Not that dogs were walked, they were just let out when they fancied. We all tolerated each other. Well, except the parrot, which actually nipped me once, to everyone's disbelief.

There were no books and no bedtime story for either Thelma or I. The Thorns never read at all and the only letters which came were for us evacuees. I don't think there was a library in the village and if so I knew no-one who used it. The only reading I did outside school was at Sunday School, where I sang the hymns. My parents had specially asked that I be sent to the Methodist Church every week and this was scrupulously observed. In fact, Thelma was also obliged to go, though her parents had made no such request and this fact was thrown in my face every time there was a particularly boring or longwinded preacher. She didn't object however, when her Methodist connections entitled her to join in the Wedding Scramble.

The Scramble was eagerly awaited by all the village children. The Auntie Betty's of the world might coo over the wedding dress and the older people sigh over a Groom who had ten days of his embarkation leave left, but we children had been told to expect showers of money. All we had to do was wave and cheer the happy couple and coins would rain down on us. We were all there far too early and in a society where nothing much ever happened, the wait was interminable. At last however, the newly weds arrived at the top of the steps and the Groom, handsome in his uniform, threw coppers into the waiting crowd. Horror of horrors however, you had to jump and compete for the coins. Everyone pushed forward and yelled. Huge boys of nine or ten leaped high into the air and caught practically each one, while the odd penny which did fall to the ground could only be picked up at the risk of having your fingers trampled on by the shoes and clogs.

I decided to withdraw. I'd never had much pocket money but I wasn't so keen to have more that I was prepared to put up with the humiliation involved in the Scramble. I had to explain this to the wedding party who, I think, were rather offended that their generosity was not considered worth the trouble.

I quite enjoyed Church, though it irritated me when others called it chapel. For weeks I was the centre of a gossiping crowd as I explained how I had been the last person to see Mrs Wilson alive. Well, almost the last. Mrs Wilson had been sitting along the pew from me when she felt ill and had squeezed passed me saying "Excuse me" before going out into the vestry where she had died before the doctor could be fetched. I not only enjoyed the celebrity status this gave me, but I felt I had had a brush with infinity. My regret was that I hadn't known till afterwards and I did think God might have given me a premonition.

Several children were fascinated by the fact that my parents had made a special request that I be sent to Church. They wanted to know why. But I too was fascinated by the fact that they didn't go to church at all. Presumably, I had known children in Newcastle who didn't go but I had never had a conversation about it. The amazing thing was that these children despised Methodists. They were sure that proper church was better. When I asked why, they could only think of the Sunday School outings and were trapped into making extravagant claims for the Parish Church outing. This caused me considerable prayer and heart searching and I awaited the two Saturdays the following summer with trepidation. The Methodists had a satisfactory, though not exciting outing, but the next week the weather was so bad that the Anglicans had to cancel, so I felt God had managed that most tactfully. The implied superiority of the others had so perturbed me that I raised the matter at home. I certainly understood that more was at stake than an outing. The Thorns were very impartial and said that one religion was probably as good as another, but parents knew what was best. They then amazed me by adding that they themselves preferred the Parish Church. This set off a major inquiry from me as to why then they never went there. I wonder what they thought of this interrogation from a six-year old and whether they sensed my doubts about them?

My doubts and unease about the Thorns' spiritual status, along with my suspicions about their encouragement of drunkenness never lasted long, however. Life was really concerned with going to school or out to play or catching the baker on Tuesdays and Thursdays, to get a cake each, before he drove off to the station and caused me to walk a mile there and a mile back between school and tea. Both Thelma and I felt safe in Tebay and if there was any advantage to be gained by going to the Parish Church it was more than outweighed by the sanctity I was no doubt acquiring by my regular Methodist attendances.

Auntie was very firm about who we could play with in the village. Most school friends were alright, but when I told her with reverence, that Margery sat on the toilet with the door open and invited everyone to look at her tummy because she had no navel, she expressed disapproval and I was told to have nothing to do with her. In fact, I was to turn my eyes away. On no account was I to keep the door open when I was in. The toilets had caused me some worry as they were outside and to ask to go during lesson time brought down Mrs Little's full fury on you. I remember being shaken like a rat in front of the whole class and I never asked again. I did keep away from Margery during lesson time, but everyone met in the toilets, so I asked several times for another look. She always obliged until one day she refused point-blank. Perhaps she was fed up with me or perhaps her mother had warned her against me. I was a great tell-tale-tit and the whole village no doubt knew of my amazement that she had no bellybutton. Once, during the winter, the toilets froze completely and we spent the first lesson despairing about how we could hang on till lunch time. Fortunately nature was not stretched so far, as a man appeared with a blow lamp to save the situation. The attractions of Margery faded for me, though later I wondered if she had had the opportunity to show Fred her unique tummy.

There were two sisters who caused Auntie some unease. The younger, Ruby, was about my age and she had asked me to her house to play. I went off with warnings in my ears about I don't know what.

"You're not to go inside."

"Why not?"

"Never mind. Just don't go in."

"What will I say if she asks me in?"

At this Auntie hesitated as she no doubt knew that whatever she said would soon be generally known.

"Well don't go in if there's anyone else there."

"Why not? Who else might be there? Won't Ruby's Mam be there? Can't I see her? What's she done?"

The conversation faded to meaningless silences, shakes of the head and tightened lips. Auntie Betty contributed the odd half laugh. This put Ruby's house on a par with the bar and the snug, but I was older now and Ruby wasn't terrifying, so the prohibition didn't seem too dangerous. Of course I went in. I was too well drilled in politeness to refuse a courteous invitation. To my amazement the kitchen was large and light and spotless and had a huge fire. The whole room was warm and there was no need to sit over the hearth. This indicated a generosity of spirit which put both Auntie and my mother to shame, but I did wonder if this extravagance with coal hinted at secret sympathies with Hitler.

Horrors of horrors, Ruby's Mam did come in. Now I was caught, but once she had reassured me about her national loyalties and that there was no-one else in the house, I relaxed. I had faith in the reasonableness of Auntie and later repeated all the conversations, to her in reassurance that no monster lived there. Ruby showed me all her jewellery and I think she liked having such an appreciative audience, so I was invited several times. It was a great novelty to be with a girl who didn't have to go out to play but could actually stay in the house in fair weather. However, I got tired of looking at her jewellery, even the string of pure pearls, so the friendship was not a lengthy one.

Ruby's sister May also was distrusted by Auntie. She was Thelma's friend, but she was nearly fourteen and Auntie said very definitely that that was too old. Thelma persisted in being friendly with her and they had to make elaborate arrangements about meeting, and go to places where no-one would see them. Thelma brought back great handfuls of bluebells at every mealtime and spun tales of going for walks. Auntie was most distrustful as no-one in Tebay went for walks, certainly no ten year-old, so she vented some of her concern on the bluebells. Firm strictures were made about not bringing any more home. We had used all the vases and we were picking too many. And now she mentioned it, we were pulling them up, not picking them and this would mean they wouldn't come up next year. I certainly didn't like to think of myself as a slaughterer of bluebells, though I hadn't picked nearly as many as Thelma, so I only picked a few in the next day or two. I remember anxiously waiting for the next year to check whether I had killed them off for ever.

But my shame didn't just extend to bluebells. Thelma continued to see May and tell lies about where she had been. Auntie must have had a good idea and various threats were made to deter her. Nothing worked. At last came the worst threat imaginable.

"If you go out with May again you won't go to the circus." I don't know if Thelma was tremendously loyal or whether she and May had a tremendously good time; or both, but even this threat did not deter her. I certainly felt excluded. I was also feeling self-righteous about having practically stopped picking bluebells and so, when on circus day Thelma was late for dinner and Auntie was wondering where she was, I told on her.

The shame of that is with me fifty years later. Thelma did miss the circus and was put to bed for the rest of the day. She had learned her lesson and as far as I know she never went out with May again. What on earth was the matter with May we never knew, but we did now know that some people were beyond the pale. And it was something to do with being a bad girl. Neither of us wanted to be bad girls.

I had looked forward to the circus for weeks and thought my happiness would be complete when it came. Wilf had got tickets for us and it was the highlight of his leave. Not only did the actual day arrive, but now I was going to have Wilf all to myself. The first cloud appeared before we even got into the tent. I was amazed to find that Wilf thought Auntie should not have punished Thelma so harshly. It appeared that he didn't think much of my tale-telling either. As everyone at the circus asked after Thelma and had to be told she was in bed as a punishment, my self-confidence quickly crumbled. I thought people looked at me as if they knew I had been responsible. Gradually, and with increasingly awful stomach lurches, it dawned on me that I would have to go home afterwards and that Thelma would know what I had done. The thought of that was appalling. I had been looking at the acts twice as hard so that I could tell Thelma all about them, but now I could hardly take them in as I was so worried about the consequences of my action. An unquiet conscience is death to circuses.

Thelma was exhausted with sobbing when I crept shame-facedly into the bedroom, but I was a relief to the monotony so she welcomed me back. To my amazement she bore me no grudge. I confessed that I had told on her and that it was my fault she'd missed the circus. She indicated that I'd really had no option if Auntie had insisted and so we were friends again. Actions like that make saints. Thelma never went out with May again and there was no more conversation about her that I ever heard. I was too busy enjoying my relief from guilt to wonder how Thelma coped with this double bereavement.

The bedroom which saw such grief, such shame and such forgiveness on that occasion, saw and heard many confidences. We talked about Newcastle which interested no-one and getting the cane at school which interested everyone. Thelma had had it once or twice and said it wasn't too bad, which reassured me when it was my turn. The bedroom itself was at the end of a long corridor so was rarely visited, and it was very cold in winter. Apart from washing only the bits that showed I took to getting into bed with all my clothes on except my top layer. It really was less trouble, as well as warmer to get in wearing a vest, a liberty bodice, thick knickers and long, lisle-thread stockings. It was the stockings that were the give-away. By Wednesday they were covered with little white balls of fluff. By Thursday the teacher at school commented and by Friday Auntie had heard on the grapevine. I had brought shame on Auntie's care - nobody thought of blaming Auntie Betty - and I had to stand at the kitchen sink to wash the stockings; while I listened to a lengthy tirade on how unjust the world was in general and what a burden I was in particular.

At least after that we were given a hot water bottle. That was not the godsend we thought it was going to be as Thelma and I found it difficult to share. I went to bed first as the youngest so had the bottle when it was really hot, but Thelma said I should give it to her when she came up as her part of the bed was still icy. Lengthy negotiations ensued resulting in an arrangement that I would have, and indeed keep, the bottle to myself, but I would lie on her half until she came to bed and then surrender the warm space. It was a pyrrhic victory however, as I got terrible chilblains with putting my bare feet on the bottle each night. When I had problems putting my shoes on I was told not to be such a cry-baby. I had another spell of moral superiority when a chilblain burst and everyone looked askance at Auntie; and for the only time ever I was allowed to stay off school until I could get my shoe on again.

It was a terrible winter and the talk was regularly of farm workers who hadn't got home some nights or to work next day. One girl who lived way up the fells wasn't able to come to school. At first I thought she was skiving off, but when I realized just how serious the situation was, I began to feel guilty. I had taken a great dislike to her because she had a receding, dimpled chin and I used to watch it when she wasn't looking. In view of the seriousness of her isolation, and she was away for many weeks, I began to take an interest in her and even thought of her quite kindly, but when the thaw came and she returned, her chin was unaffected and my dislike returned.

Thelma said she was quite nice, but I could not get past that chin.

School was good. Our own Newcastle teachers left after about a week to my amazement, as I had thought they would stay for ever. Mrs Little took over and I was relieved to find that she was quite kind though firm, despite being Church and living at the wrong end of the village. Her husband was a Captain in the army and never seen. I was amazed to find she was married and thought to care for her husband yet taught in school. Presumably, she was the first married woman to go out to work that I had heard of. Or else she was the first teacher who hadn't gone into a drawer once school was finished. It was she who gave me the cane, though I didn't hold it against her. We were learning to write in ink and she was tired of the mess we were making. The crossed nibs and the inkwells with bits of blotting paper drove us to distraction and we all found it terribly difficult; but she had thirty or forty of us and was obviously at the end of her tether.

"Anyone else who makes a blot will get the cane!"

The cane was always handy and she walked round to check our work. Horror of horrors, a huge blot appeared on my work even though I was doing most of the things she told us to do. To the front I had to go and hold my hand out. The disgrace was the worst part as it didn't hurt very much. By the time I got home from school

Auntie already knew, but I never did work that one out.

In an effort to redeem myself I offered to look after some tadpoles for the holiday. This was more to ingratiate myself with Mrs Little than any interest in the tadpoles. The jam jar was duly given to me but I was sick of them before I even got home. You had to walk slowly as the jar was full to the brim and endure the comments of those whose kind offers had been rejected. To the boys, who thought I would not be able to cope when the tadpoles became frogs, I had no answer. Not because they were right but because I really didn't believe they would ever become frogs.

Having got them home and having been ordered out of the kitchen with them, I put them on a window ledge and promptly forgot all about them. Two weeks later school began again and my stomach suddenly lurched towards my feet as I remembered those tadpoles. The end of the world appeared as I sped to the windowsill to check on my charges. The world stood still. Every one was dead. I shook the jar and the world moved a little as the tadpoles appeared to swim nearer the surface. It stopped again as they sank to the bottom. Never, before or since, have I prayed so hard for a resurrection. Nor dreaded going back to school as I did. Auntie was an angel from heaven when she said I need not carry the corpses back with me, and Mrs Little just a little less than God, when she shrugged and pardoned me and said she wasn't terribly surprised. I wasn't even the only tadpole slaughterer - though one boy had brought back his jam jar and we duly admired the backlegs which had grown. My image of myself as a trustworthy and somewhat superior person was severely dented, so I was able to reject the idea that had I had a one pound jam jar, instead of a two pound one, generations of frogs might now be alive.

The Tebay children expected no better from us evacuees. We didn't know the difference between great tits and coal tits or know the witches prayer, or indeed any of the rhymes you skipped or whipped your top to. We couldn't walk far or climb the fells quickly and we had white, unhealthy faces. They repeated with relish tales of bad behaviour about this one and that one and weren't surprised when one by one we went home.

I too went home. I was never homesick but I came to realize that I was a serious cause of embarrassment to the Thorns and my parents were unhappy to have me away any longer. I had seen them several times a year as one or other came through to visit. These were ordeals, as Auntie begrudged any hospitality even to the odd customer. Mr Thorn had to coax her into making a cheese sandwich for a salesman, who hadn't eaten all day, and he didn't dare say anything when she took his ration book and cut out his whole week's cheese ration. My father had a motor bike and I worried all morning through Sunday School as ghastly tales abounded of travellers going astray on long journeys without signposts. When he did arrive he talked of the bad time he had had coming over Shap. I didn't know what Shap was, but I worried about it all during the evening as he drove back. He was given lunch; but it was made clear that in future he must bring sandwiches.

My mother came by the bus which was occasionally laid on. She had to get up at some unimaginably early hour, walk to the centre of Newcastle and then travel for a long time to reach the village. Once there, my joy knew no bounds despite the sad fact that conversation was somewhat difficult after a gap of many months. She had brought her own sandwiches and ate them at the dining room table with the rest of us, but she wasn't offered a cup of tea. Despite the fact that we all had a cup to finish the Sunday dinner she was very definitely excluded. She was very unhappy, and this one failure in courtesy was to colour both our recollections of the Thorns.

Mam and Dad had always stressed that I just had to say the word and I could come home. This had made me impervious to taunts from school friends that my parents were glad to be rid of me but there were taunts that I knew were true.

"Ruth Kirkley's got nits in her hair."

Everyone seemed to know. And I was the one who got picked on which seemed most unjust as I knew perfectly well I was not the only one. I'd got them from Louise, a girl at the wrong end of the village, who had called at the pub one day on the way home from school as it was raining very heavily. Auntie told me to lend her my cape which hung handily just inside the door. Now I loved that cape of dark blue with its hood attached and I certainly didn't want to lend it to anyone, never mind Louise. I hummed and ha'ad and made excuses until Auntie was most annoyed, but I couldn't cope with the situation of saying out loud that she had a dirty head. So I gave in and Louise went off in my cape. And that was that.

Eventually the Thorns realized that I had nits and blamed me. I was accused of being a dirty girl. The indignation caused by unjust accusations (I didn't count my feet which no-one ever saw), made me most vocal and I certainly told Auntie that it was her fault as she had made me give my cape to Louise. Whether I had hurt Auntie irreparably I don't know, but she suddenly remembered that Auntie Betty was supposed to be in charge of me and Auntie Betty was commanded to comb out the nits. So began the nightly ritual of me leaning over a newspaper spread over the kitchen table while Auntie Betty combed my hair with a small tooth comb. Sometimes she scored, sometimes she didn't. Sometimes a real live louse fell out and scampered away to universal shouting. She got discouraged and I got a sore scalp and we were obviously losing the battle. People no longer cared to have me around and in a weak moment I wrote in my weekly letter that I would like to go home.

My parents made the arrangements at once.

One familiar world was lost to me for ever.

CHAPTER THREE

SOUTH SEA ISLAND BLUE

There was something called The Scholarship which every child had to sit. How you did in this affected your whole life, so ambitious parents began to worry at least a year beforehand. It cannot really have been intended that the children from our suburb should have every disadvantage, yet we were all moved to a different school six months before the exam. So at ten I had to cope with a tram ride which took me only halfway, a long walk, a new teacher, a male Head and a totally different type of pupil. What can have possessed the Education Committee I cannot imagine. We all hated our new School, were divided into several different classes and really had no sense of belonging at all. The sums we did were all about baths being filled from taps at one end and emptied from the other and we were expected to find out how long it took to fill it. As if anyone cared, or indeed, ever had a bath totally filled with water. Questions about overflow when you got in or about balmy people who wasted water on such a scale, were considered cheeky.

There was bullying here which made my life very unhappy for a few weeks. I also had my first encounter with pupils who had failed the Scholarship and who therefore stayed on at the same school until they were fourteen. They seemed to me to have no worthwhile future either at the school or in later life. This must have been my mother's conditioning and her way of motivating me but obviously, even at ten, I had absorbed the English custom of writing-off seventy-five per cent of my age-group as failures. What disappointed maternal hopes it concealed, I didn't recognise until many years later.

The school did bring some awareness of tragedy in others' lives.

I had known people whose sons had been killed in the war and indeed, one young man I had known personally, but that had been far away in Europe. This was in my own world. The Art teacher was there one week for the lesson, but dead before the next. My class teacher was away for a few days and on her return we learned she had attempted suicide. Guilt was well established at ten so I was ashamed I hadn't noticed any special sign or signal or been nicer to them.

The day of the examination was very cold indeed but we all turned up to sit in the hall for three separate sessions. There was one Maths test, one English test and a nice one full of puzzles. I wrote an essay on the given title "After the Storm", which was truly exhausting as I swept and mended and called in repair men and wrote many pages filled with domestic detail. I was rather disappointed with my efforts as I usually prided myself on a more imaginative approach, but I was careful with commas, full-stops and speech marks.

There were several months to wait for the results and then an interview at my first choice school. There were more tests and an interview with the Headmistress. Then there was more waiting, made more difficult as others heard before I did that they had been successful. But the acceptance letter came eventually and the fees to be paid were manageable, so I was in.

My new secondary school was altogether different and I loved it from the beginning. There were no boys, different teachers for every subject and a brown and gold uniform that I was really proud to wear. We all wore hats and gloves whenever we were outside and woe betide the girl who was seen eating in public. Hats those days had high crowns, but you weren't allowed to put a tuck in the back. Mine had an elastic on as I cycled, but on a windy day you had to have one hand hanging onto your hat. Later, open defiance came over that hat tuck.

We had to provide our own textbooks and Mam was alarmed at the length of the list. Fortunately, it was wartime so nearly everything was out of print. During the year a new law said schools had to provide the books so this was a load off our minds. I think the staff thought this would mark the end of any respect for books but that did not happen. A new worry emerged as we all had to cover our own and I had problems, as we didn't have any wallpaper, the accepted medium. I think I used the paper the groceries came in, but often found it difficult to keep the ends down in those pre-sellotape days.

French was a new subject and algebra and geometry, but so were gym and science. New subjects, new teachers, new classmates and senior pupils, who at eighteen, were quite grown up. I seemed always unsure and timid and anxious to do the right thing and it took nearly a year before I could relax. There had been absolutely no preparation for this tremendous change. To add to everyone's discomfiture, my mother was anxious to know what everyone's father did, and as someone's father was the Town Clerk, another the owner of a department store, several were doctors, one a university lecturer, I had to cope with a social hierarchy that few others were even aware of.

There was a different colour for each best book and a rough book that I didn't know what to do with. There had to be silence in the cloakrooms and prefects to keep us in order. We were supposed to change our shoes to indoor shoes the moment we came into the building, but nobody bothered about it at Break, so it can't have really mattered. There were prayers every day and unreliable bells which a selected Fifth Year pupil rang every forty minutes. Not that the staff had a great selection as few of us had watches. There was milk at Break, originally two pence ha'penny a week, but soon to be free. There were dinners at eight pence but I didn't sample them for a long time. The crowd from our area all went home for dinner: it took twenty-five minutes to get home, twenty to get back, so you had fifteen minutes in the house.

It wasn't till the Summer term that we relaxed and began to get order marks for misbehaviour. The first one or two were most shaming but once you'd signed the Order book a few times nobody minded very much. Those of us who travelled on the same bus each day must have felt we could cope with some social life, so founded the Mystery Marauders. We met on Tuesdays in members' garages and swore secrecy, elected a president and a secretary and did a lot of talking. We were at that funny age between playing and conversation, so felt we wanted the first, but should enjoy the second. At some point we learned the true meaning of Marauders and had to change to Mystery Maidens; a change I was much against as I thought that we could make the word mean what we wanted it to mean, and someone had broken their oath by even discussing it with anyone else. Our meetings went on over the whole summer and only came to an end when the dark evenings came.

School became familiar. I was a member of a group of friends and liked everyone in my form. Teachers and other pupils revolved round us to provide education; some were pleasanter or more noticeable than others, no-one was really nasty and yet much of our conversation was about personalities. There probably wasn't enough variety to teach us about the more unpleasant side of human nature, so we had to learn that from literature. Over the years Toad, Loki, Pau-Puk-Keewis, the Macbeths, Angel, Emma, Hamlet, Piers Gaveston, revealed weaknesses and ruthlessnesses that never seemed to surprise me and who made my world no less comfortable as they came to bad ends - or at least, awkward middles. And anyway, they were all in books. There were few moral dilemmas for me. Adultery, fornication, bullying in all its forms, stealing, jealousy, wasting money, going your own sweet way, breaking your word were all wrong. Unconscious trampling on others wouldn't have counted had I even noticed it. I hoped to be liked but never expected to be loved and sensed that grand passions led to grand agonies. Grand passions existed in literature but not in my family or the families of those I knew. I had my life arranged quite tidily.

Intellectually one grew. Socially too, up to a point. There were parties nearly every Saturday where we played Hunt the Thimble, Musical Chairs and Jumbled Letters among other things and always finished up with Murder. The tea was a highlight and we regularly sat down to a tremendous spread of cakes. The preparations for one's own party took ages and involved considerable worry over the purchases of prizes. There were no imported entertainers and even mothers were only allowed around at tea-time. But we happily competed for combs, nail files, hair slides and small notebooks.

Talking to one's contemporaries was easy as we mainly talked about school and the people we knew in common. Talking to adults was very different. Although we gossiped about teachers and wondered about their private lives, the thought of asking them about holidays or weekends never crossed our minds. Even at seventeen, teachers were another species. My years in Secondary School coincided with the great Labour Government of 1945-51, yet I never took an informed part in any conversation about the new National Health Scheme. All I heard were snippets from Doctors' daughters, who regularly commented on the Government's failure to pay salaries on time. Nationalisation was not a mystery, as I read about it in the papers, but I had no opinion about it. People made remarks but I never heard two people discussing it reasonably. In fact, it was many years before I understood that you didn't have to argue when you disagreed and that there was no winning or losing.

There was a boys' school opposite to us and although we used their swimming pool and had invitations to Chamber Music concerts, we had no ordinary contact. You didn't even see a boy and girl from the two schools walking along the street together. I wouldn't have known what to talk about had a boy joined me. I would have wanted to appear witty and charming but would probably just have been silent. I knew nothing about sport or radio programmes and rarely went to the pictures, yet I seemed to think these were the suitable topics. The only thing I felt I could talk about was religion but that didn't seem appropriate.

I did know quite a lot of boys. I had always gone to Church and was thrilled when a Youth Club was started. A small group of us, aged about twelve or thirteen, had a good time visiting police stations, fire stations, castles nearby and the seaside. Later, there probably were about sixty or seventy of us in the Senior Section and we remained friends for several years. Marriages resulted from this Club and the Methodist Church got an excellent reputation for lively young people. So much so, that young offenders were ordered to attend by the Court. They no doubt thought it very tame, however. We rarely told our mothers as they would suspect some sort of infectious corruption, but the visitors rarely lasted long enough to corrupt any of us; a disappointment as we would have liked to know what temptations we were expected to withstand.

As I grew older nearly all my social life was at Church. I enjoyed the Club, the Choir and the weekly dances. I was in everything that went on - at least, everything that girls were included in. Some of the boys disappeared for ages into the Billiard room and girls were not welcome there. I had no desire to play billiards, but resented the fact that they had a room virtually to themselves. My problem was that my school life and my church life were totally separate and there was no overlap. I had a feeling that my school friends would look down on my Church friends because they didn't go to such a grand school. One boy from the Club went to the School opposite so would have been acceptable had he been a year older and a bit taller, but the others, sadly, went to the local Grammar School which in our arrogance, we barely acknowledged.

What a pity that I cared so much what school friends thought. Their thoughts were rarely expressed in words but I understood body language before the term was invented, and was alert to every nuance in speech and glance. I was far more relaxed with Club friends.

Boyfriends came and went and I spent a lot of my teenage years wishing my life away. If I was to see Raymond on Friday, Monday to Friday was just a waste of time to be dreamed through. If Kenneth was taking me to the pictures on Saturday, life wasn't worth living until then. Some days became highlights when I was on a peak, the rest were full of time to be killed. Boyfriends in the early days just meant boys you liked very much as I certainly wasn't allowed to go out with them. Nobody else did either so this wasn't any real deprivation. Most of the time I was in a group of Church friends so the last dance or the walk home was important. When the Youth Club ended for the summer we were at a loose end and did our best to enjoy the walk through Jesmond Dene. The problem was that unless you were really going steady, boys and girls walked separately. Each, of course, was aware of the other and remarks were flung across, but you could neither talk properly to your friends nor to the boys.

I was sixteen before I was allowed to go out with Kenneth. Our parents knew each other and I think my mother was nervous of being challenged by his mother, so it was agreed that I could accept his next invitation. Once the hurdle of the first date was over we saw a lot of each other. Those were the days a boy walked you home after the evening function so, sadly, you were always looking forward to the end of your date.

School was generally happy. The work was easy if very boring. Most teachers talked a lot of the time so I just switched off. I could read it up in the text book later. First year Latin was fun, as the teacher used games and competitions and you ran to the front if you were in the first few to finish. English was fun as we read aloud a lot, or took parts in plays. As I was Hiawatha, Rosalind, Mole, Demeter, the wife in The Doll's House, Edward II, Ophelia, and many others, the lessons did much to encourage my self-confidence. I never inquired what it did for those who were constantly passed over. Maths was the best because you were active the whole time and didn't have to learn or remember anything. Latin, after the good teacher left, and French and German were just hours to be got through. I never really expected to need to write French and that was all we did.

Science was a total horror. The teacher was a thoroughly bad-tempered woman, who shouted quite unnecessarily, and threw chalk at you. Once I had my Best Book thrown at me as she objected to the colour of the ink I'd used. I had admired South Sea Island Blue in the Post Office for some time, so when our bottle of ink ran out I got the money to buy it. As soon as I got it home I knew there would be trouble. It was bright turquoise. The picture on the front and the reality had little in common. There was no money for a second bottle so it had to be used up. Ever since, I've used black.

I still haven't forgotten or really forgiven that teacher for her contempt for me and my work, but at least I learned a few things about iron filings and lenses and learned to draw a plan of the wiring of an electric bell. We never saw an electric bell and there wasn't one at school or at home, so it was purely academic. I didn't learn anything much from the next Science teacher and this time the contempt was mine. She looked about ninety and dressed accordingly. Her voice was a whisper and I think she was frightened of us. Her subject was biology and she couldn't believe that some of us didn't know the names of any flowers but for the commonest, and didn't particularly want to know. We did drawings of pistils and stamens but the only wildlife that got inside the lab were leaves and beans. It took nearly thirty years for an interest in plants and animals to develop.

In the 1940's the only acceptable careers for girls - careers as opposed to jobs - were teaching and nursing, so several generations of pupils suffered instruction from women who hated both them and the daily grind. I expect they also felt guilty about it so we probably had to suffer for that too.

There was good teaching in some subjects and many happy memories and successes, but it is the unusual and the unpleasant that stay in the memory. Like the day in gym when Rosemary dislocated both her shoulders and her screams of pain echoed through the building and down the years. Or the time the Headmistress came to watch our lesson - as there had been complaints from a neighbour about a teacher's language in the playground. The time I had to tell the English teacher that I couldn't afford the three pence it cost to join the Junior Library for the term, and the satisfaction I had from wondering whether that had anything to do with it being made totally free next term.

My mother had strange views about reading. She herself loved a good story but felt guilty if she sat down to read for anything over half-an-hour. She only allowed me to have one book a week and this was a real anguish for me. What desolation there was on Saturday afternoon when I'd finished my book and had a week's boredom to face. Reading was a joy in itself as well as an escape from a dreary home. At my Secondary School I hit on the plan to take out collected works and my life was transformed. Of course, at home reading had to be dropped at a second's notice to help in the house or go on an errand - but a world of magic was waiting for me. I am one of the few people who has read her way through Andrew Lang's Red Book of Fairy Stories, the Blue Book, the Green Book, the Yellow, the Purple, the Orange and whatever other shade he published. I read about whole dynasties of people and followed Sue Barton from Probationer to Matron through twelve volumes. I read collected animal stories, collected adventure stories and a year's issues of Punch bound into one volume. Father Brown and Sherlock Holmes lasted me nearly a fortnight each and the resultant indigestion meant a small sigh of relief that I could turn to next week's book, held smugly in reserve.

This lasted until I was nearly twelve when Mam dropped the embargo. It happened after a School At Home, so presumably a teacher had interceded for me. Thereafter, I had more normal reading patterns. We had no working radio until I was about fourteen and few visitors to the house, except my grandmother each Friday for tea, so some occupation was vital.

There were concerts and plays at school, a great selection of clubs and a small range of sports. I was in everything except the sports. I hated team games and as we merely copied the philosophy of boys' schools, we didn't have much else. Tennis I found hard going as the only racquet I had was my father's and it was almost too heavy to lift. The School Choir was a weekly pleasure and I enjoyed that enormously. I think we were very good. Certainly we won lots of awards at the North of England Musical Festival but when we went to audition at Newcastle B.B.C. we were turned down. We sang too much like Young Ladies. They said listeners would not believe we were a choir of schoolgirls. Whether that was the truth or a charming way of saying "No", I have no idea, but it was an honourable way to be rejected.

I enjoyed swimming, even though the water was icy, and took part in several water ballets, but my real love was ballroom dancing. The problem with this was that you needed a partner. A boy a little taller than yourself was essential, someone who could actually dance and had some sense of rhythm. In those days I tended to believe what people said and felt continually diminished by a general male contempt of dancing. I don't think I realized it hid inadequacy. Anyway, dancing with another girl was socially unacceptable and as there was no money to go to a dancing class where I might have met other keen dancers, I never got far.

All my secondary years were spent with post war shortages. Clothes were still on coupons, so equipping me with my initial uniform took the year's supply of three generations. Not that the school relaxed any of its demands. Sweets were rationed for most of the time but I had so little money that I never used up my monthly ration anyway. Three pence a week brought two ounces of the cheapest type and I used to get wine gums as they lasted the longest. Food shops had little to sell and rarely bothered to make a display. Indeed, the Butcher regularly had a window showing triangular pieces of grease proof paper hanging neatly, one from each of a row of hooks. Fish and chip shops had the windows painted white to above eye-level and wet fish shops didn't even open every day. Very few people seemed to eat fish in those days, yet it was unrationed.

The beaches were closed for several years after the end of the war, but we sometimes took a walk along the Front at the coast. There were huge rolls of barbed wire and posts stuck in the sand, but what deterred anyone from even attempting to get through, were the stories of people being blown up by mines. Some of the main streets had enormous concrete barriers which had been set up to prevent enemy tanks and which, years later, still managed to slow down traffic.

People survived a joyless period by making a virtue out of shortages. You weren't even supposed to want what you couldn't have. Since there was little money anyway, many of us grew up thinking that luxuries were not for us and that self-indulgence was, if not sinful, at least weakness.

Gradually things came into the shops in quantities that meant they weren't all sold instantly. I remember rushing home to announce that Hadrian's had biscuits that anyone could buy and being sent straight back to walk the two miles to get half-a-pound. Clothes were no longer Utility and the New Look came in with its yards of fabric and high heels. Bananas made a stealthy return and the first lucky few breathed heavily over friends, inviting them to guess what they'd had for pudding. Ice cream was made again and the Italian families who seemed to be in control, could not keep up with the enormous queues which formed as soon as the shop window opened.

Sweets came off the ration but had to go back on as those with enough money made bulk purchases. Once the supply was re-established the sweet shop windows became an absolute joy. The eye was saturated with plenty: pyramids of boiled sweets of every possible colour; jars of black bullets, humbugs, fruitellas, clove balls, mint imperials; slabs of chocolate, coconut ice and nougat stacked high; trays of fudge and home-made toffee with its own hammer, and if there was a square inch of space, it was packed with tubes of wine and fruit gums, packets of jelly babies, nets of golden coins and sticks of liquorice. The aristocrats of this sugary world were the Boxes of Chocolates, rarely on display in the window but in pride of place inside. What a world of opulence and self-indulgence was on show. For us it remained on show as there was no money to buy more, but it provided the chance to show some superiority over those who squandered their money.

Squandering money was unthinkable for us as we had so little. My father had a good, middle management job, far below his capabilities, but he'd been out of work for nine months in his mid-thirties and thereafter lost confidence to take any sort of risk. He did a job that three men took on when he eventually retired at sixty-eight. The salary seemed to be about three pounds a week when I was small, gradually edged up to five over the years and reached a triumphant one thousand a year, when last it was mentioned to me. This rise in wealth was not reflected in the house as much of it went to the Church. Getting new clothes was always a major problem so Mam and I used a dressmaker for any major item. Men and boys, of course, had to be dressed from shops. We were buying our own house which brought social cachet but no other immediate advantage. We had a family holiday each year, often in a guest house or the Factory Rest Home and we went to the News Reel every Saturday.

I didn't object to the News Reel as such, but I loathed standing in the queue in the main Newcastle street. It wasn't quite so bad if I was wearing ordinary clothes, but I had a deep sense of disgrace if I was in uniform. Not only was it infra dig to be in the queue for such a cheap show but I didn't wear my hat. I was between the devil and the deep blue sea.

People sniggered if I wore the hat but teachers told me off on Monday if I didn't. Nobody else went to the News Reel from school so there was no-one to discuss it with. Nor could I join in the discussion of this or that film.

There came a time when I'd really worked on my mother and we had a big row with my father, about us going to the pictures instead. He really thought that paying for us to go to the cheapest show in town was all he should be expected to do. His injured dignity lasted for several weeks but then he too began to enjoy the films.

This was the only time in the week that he gave to family life. He worked long hours and Saturday mornings though without extra pay and spare time was given to the Masons and the Church. Leaders Meetings, Trustee Meetings, Quarterly Meetings, L.P.M.A Meetings went on non-stop while there was Church morning and evening on Sundays and he was Superintendent of the Sunday School on Sunday afternoons. He was a Local Preacher and prepared his sermons and services very carefully. I only saw him at weekends and my mother saw little extra. I'm sure he thought he was doing God's will and he often gave deep sighs of martyrdom when his family "misunderstood" him, but really he wasn't suited to family life.

This made my mother very unhappy as she liked to have her family around her and she was quite a sociable person. As he was never there, she couldn't invite people to tea as you were supposed to be a couple to invite others. There was no spare money to do things and my mother's sole weekly outing was on a Tuesday afternoon when she went to town to look round Binns. She never bought anything. Not only was she tied to the house through lack of money, she lost all self-confidence as she was a virtual prisoner. She never went for walks, hated Church life (though she too was a religious person), and couldn't join anything as she had the two of us, and David was still small. No-one ever offered to baby-sit and she wouldn't have had anywhere to go if they had.

Over the years she got more and more bad-tempered and resentful though she was quite inarticulate and didn't know she had a problem; never mind knowing what the problem was. She took it out on my brother and me, particularly me, as I was growing away from her as I became adolescent. She resented my growing independence and the pleasant time I managed to have at school and the youth club. Life at home became a burden as I was given more and more housework to do but nothing was ever good enough. Hardly a day passed without her giving me a big whack over the head and the only time she spoke pleasantly was when there were others around. And that wasn't too often. It would be true to say that I grew to hate her.

Thus the years between twelve and seventeen were unhappy at home. There was still the loyalty which prevented me from complaining to anyone and my mother never knew I hated her, but they were dreary years in a home without fun or real conversation.

CHAPTER FOUR

INTO THE ELIZABETHAN AGE

There had been no question of me going away to university. My mother was too uneasy about the unknown area of higher education and somewhat resentful of the fact that I would not be bringing in any wages despite being seventeen. I wasn't brimming over with self-confidence either. I had no idea how to go about finding digs in another town and even less about what money I was likely to get from the Local Authority. I hoped to get something but there was a sliding scale of awards based on parental income, and as the application was completed by my father in great secrecy, I couldn't work any figures out. This must have been a problem for many first generation students: school was a world recognisable to parents but college wasn't.

I did win a City Major Scholarship valued at one hundred and fifty pounds per year. Half of this went straight to my mother for my keep and I lived on the rest. This was in fact, very little, as the Authority expected students to keep the whole grant and everyone else I knew got the whole sum.

The first lecture appalled me as an enormous booklist was dictated. I only bought four or five books in the whole three years and even then my mother couldn't refrain from commenting on the waste of money. She was very anxious that I be well dressed at college and after wearing uniform for seven years it was delightful to get into colours. I refused to keep changing every day however and fought to be reasonably informal.

The first row between us came at the end of my first week. I had about eight lectures a week, spread about rather inconveniently. When she realised that I didn't need to be in till ten some mornings I had to do my usual chores and then was expected back straight after the lecture. This meant helping with the dishes, making three beds, tidying and cleaning the upstairs rooms and washing the bathroom and lavatory floors, setting tables and being available for any shopping and cooking that was needed. This had not been expected of me at school, except at weekends, and as my mother had long since given me her own hatred of housework, I refused to do it. It meant that ever after, I was one of the earliest students in the library and I was able to do some work before lectures started.

This was in the early Fifties and the standard of lecturing had to be heard to be believed. The very first lecture was given by an unsympathetic woman with an unpronounceable name who turned out to be my tutor. Apparently a tutor was someone you went to if you had problems. She firmly announced that she hated first year students and kept grinding her teeth and giving little growls. Later she told me she didn't like women students either, so no wonder we all kept our distance.

Her first lecture, the one that was preceded by the terrifying booklist, was an account of the Barbarian invasions of the Roman Empire in the fifth and sixth centuries. She had no notes and rambled on for an hour, repeating herself, putting in tribes she'd forgotten to mention, getting quite excited about the difference between Ostrogoths and Visigoths, and suddenly swooping over to China to debate the origin of the Huns, who apparently had started the whole thing off, but who didn't get a mention till near the end. She did have the grace to say that if we found her account confusing that was because it was a very confusing period. We had all given up trying to take notes and when she left the room there was a roar of anger. This was followed by a rather glum silence as we wondered what we had let ourselves in for, for the next three years. In my first week, therefore, I realised that if I was going to learn any history I was going to learn it alone.

She set us our first essay quite soon. The whole group got a delta. No comment. No corrections. No variation. Older students roared with laughter at the dismayed group: they too had been treated to the same contemptuous treatment. I should say that I was entirely self-taught at University. Other lecturers were better but I could rarely say at the end "How interesting". I was always glad to get out.

They also had the annoying habit of not marking our essays until every last one was in. I liked to get my work done promptly, and in any case, there was so much, that if I didn't do one essay a week I couldn't keep up. But though mine was usually in on time, I would often have to wait six or seven weeks to get it back. There was then a tutorial in which the lecturer commented on what each of us had written. I couldn't remember anything I'd written by then. Others must have been the same as I don't remember any discussion, just another hour of listening to somebody talking.

I had not lived in a house where there ever was any serious discussion so I was very unsure of myself. Nor had there been much encouragement at school. Now here I was, at seventeen mixing with men for the first time and finding that quite intimidating. The boys my own age were alright, but much of the History School was made up of men in their twenties, who had done their National Service. Socially, I could cope, but I couldn't debate any historical theory with them, despite the fact that I was obviously alright on paper. This was something that I was very conscious of when teaching girls later on. Lots of families talk of little but daily matters or comment only on lightweight television programmes and girls particularly, need constant practise and encouragement.

There was a ruthless weeding out process at the end of our first year; done entirely through examinations and half the students disappeared from the Honours School into other courses. The Latin papers caused me considerable anxiety as I'd not been to more than half-a-dozen seminars. The Lecturer sat at the front, swathed in a dusty gown, and called out people's names. The named person then read a few paragraphs from the crib that went round the room. Was the man really so stupid that he didn't know? I wasn't going to waste my time on this, so had read the set books alone; some Bede, Tacitus, a book of Virgil and no proses. They were simpler than 'A' level and for the first time I actually enjoyed Latin. The exam was very straightforward, fortunately.

There was only one Lecturer in our first year who could talk logically and coherently about his subject. However, it happened to be Roman Britain with a great deal of evidence taken from pottery shards. I hated ruins and broken things and was surprised when nearly half the group chose it as their Special Period.

My first year had taught me that I had only myself to rely on and that the whole superstructure of professors, readers and lecturers was entirely superfluous. No wonder the universities in the Sixties were so turbulent. And thank goodness they were. I wish we had had the confidence to demand even modest standards of teaching.

Second year was better. I enjoyed working entirely on my own. There was a tremendous workload, but my mother had begun to understand that reading was work, even though she didn't consider I should find it tiring. There was one good Lecturer who could actually communicate. I was secure in that I knew I would get some sort of degree at the end and I was having a splendid social life.

I began to enjoy being a student.

There were lots of societies to join and dances and debates. I did some swimming, joined the Methodist Society and gave my wholesale support to Rag Week. This annual fund raising event did raise an enormous amount of money for sufferers of diseases I often hadn't heard of till then. We dressed up and sat on lorries which drove first round Newcastle then round half of Northumberland. We had some political theme which involved the then cabinet and a guillotine and all I can remember is that I was Barbara Castle, and had to wear a huge name badge round my neck as I looked nothing like her. There were shows and cabarets and nobody did a stroke of work.

I fell in love with Geoff who kept quiet about the fact that he was already engaged to someone else, and was devastated when he eventually confessed. I rebounded into a relationship with Mick, not realising that I was using him, so that had to be finished quite painfully, a year later. I went from heights to depths and back again frequently. The whole three years stretched me emotionally and I watched it happening to myself. I was so conditioned to ladylike behaviour though, that it never occurred to me to tell Geoff what I thought of him or to fight for him; I just accepted his rejection. I actually told him that it didn't matter. What I was saying was that I didn't matter.

Looking back, it seems incredible that I could not talk about my feelings. I certainly knew what I felt but I had been conditioned to subordinate them to other factors: to what was suitable, to what was ladylike and to what I thought was inevitable. It never occurred to me to take the initiative. Unknowingly, I co-operated in society's judgement of women, that we were objects.

I had friends who were men and I treated them entirely differently; arguing, disagreeing and sticking up for myself. Martyrdom was reserved for a different type of relationship and though the unhappiness was devastating and always present, it was a deepening experience from which I emerged more mature. As an evacuee during the war I understood that nobody liked me very much and this confirmed it. You still go on living and it's useful knowledge for a teacher. Even more useful for a Head.

During my first year, King George Vl died. We had not known he was ill and I remember the stillness which fell over the campus as the news went round, the moment frozen at the news of the death of a man I'd never thought of as an individual. He'd just been around. I remember the long narrow passage way between the Hut where I'd been to one of my few Latin 'lessons' and the Union building and the clear calm morning. I had a sense of unbelief. The King was an institution who had always been there. Stuttering, kindly, hard-working, unexciting; we all liked him and took him totally for granted. Now suddenly we missed him.

The next few days we saw the new Queen return, with red eyes, from Africa. News Reels showed her coming down the aircraft steps dressed in black from head to foot and everyone was rather horrified to know she had taken mourning clothes on a State visit. That was taking conscientiousness too far, and I was also somewhat contemptuous of the news having to be given to her, by her husband and not direct.

Very few people had television sets, but every cinema showed the News at length and there were many News Reels. These were small cinemas which gave shows lasting about an hour and here we saw the lying-in-state, the Proclamation of the New Queen and the funeral. People seemed far less critical in those days and though I thought the waist-length veils worn by the two Queens and Princess Margaret ridiculous, as I'm sure others did, no-one mentioned them at the time.

A gloom hung over everyone, not helped by the dirge like music played non-stop on the radio and the reverent tones and hushed voices of announcers.

Life of course, goes on and gaiety emerged, punctuated by the odd stab of guilt at forgetting others' misery. As the months went on and preparations proceeded for the coronation we had the most amazing press hyperbole about the New Elizabethan Age and the Young Queen. It began to appear that the post-war problems were really over and colour, pageantry and prosperity were to start for all. In a rush of enthusiasm, a group of us determined to go to London for the coronation.

We travelled overnight and then went to sit by the roadside in Park Lane, on the park side not too far from the mobile toilets. We had heard that the Mall was full even before we left on the overnight excursion train. It meant that there would be no real action until after the ceremony so we settled ourselves to wait for the return procession which was something like half-past three. We had our first experience of a London crowd and didn't stop talking to those around us all day. There were loud speakers on the trees so we could hear the commentary on the Queen's departure from the palace and Jean Metcalfe's excited comment, "The Queen spoke to me. Did you hear her? She spoke to me". We laughed but were impressed with this evidence of her humanity. We laughed at everything. We clapped and cheered every soldier and policeman near us, every late arriving spectator in the tiered seats opposite and everyone of the hundreds of chaps selling patriotic favours. We cheered when we heard that Hillary had reached the summit of Everest, even though our good humour didn't hide the suspicion that the news had been deliberately delayed until this special morning.

The police moved us up at eight-thirty, so we had to stand and that wasn't quite so good, but the crowds were immense by then and presumably, it was as much to save us from the possibility of being crushed, as to get more people in. The queues for the loos became immense and you could bank on a half-hour wait. Friends kept your place however, so it was a change of scenery.

The first false alarm gave me some idea of the power of the crowd. It surged forward and we lost the advantageous position we thought ours, by right of length of stay and distance of origin. However, things weren't too bad and we used our elbows to good effect in later surges. No good getting too uptight trying to see a mounted policeman.

The Procession eventually came. We had no doubt that this was the real thing as we could hear the tremendous cheering like a tidal roar further down Park Lane and coming towards us. We cheered everything again: the Guards, the politicians, the visiting dignitaries, Queen Salote of Tonga who was one of the few to extend to us the courtesy of an open carriage despite the shower of rain, the foreign Royals, the Gloucesters, the Kents, the Sovereign's escort and finally the coronation coach itself. I remember staring absolutely greedily into the coach to burn every detail of the Queen, her regalia and the vehicle into my memory for ever. And it is still clear in my memory. The Queen's beautiful skin, the orb in a rest and not in her hand, the crown which did seem to flash as she turned to look in our direction and the violet of the robe. Much bluer than I had expected. The coach itself was superb and I can remember whole painted scenes, though I can't remember what they were scenes of.

The moment the coach passed, the crowd dispersed. Not after a minute, immediately. The good humour and temporary friends were all gone and the grim business of getting home began. The streets of London were packed and we were not only in the crush on the way to the Tube station but in danger of being run down by several carloads of peers. They all looked totally exhausted and somewhat doll-like in their robes. We went out to my aunt's house in the suburbs for a meal and we saw highlights of the ceremony on television. Lots of people had bought television sets for the coronation and it was an absolute thrill to be right inside the Abbey.

During the evening we saw the superb fireworks and danced in the street as we made our way back to King's Cross. We felt we'd been part of history as well as students of it.

The bulk of a student's life is hard work. The image is different and there are people who waste time but most of us did work very hard. The period before Finals is very stressful as a failure here means you have wasted the last three years. Your mind might have broadened and deepened, but you would have nothing tangible to show for it. So there was even more work and it was the quantity rather than the difficulty that was a heavy burden. I had a craze for getting up at five in the morning to get in three hours before leaving to go to get my favourite corner seat in the Library. I don't know that I achieved very much as I was so tired in the evening that I had to go to bed early. During the day everyone sounded relaxed and implied that they weren't working hard. This was in case they were thought to be swots. I doubt if we fooled anyone. What with working hard, continuing a good social life and giving blood regularly I got so thin and was so tired that my mother took me off to Gretna Green for a long weekend.

In the hotel there was a Scottish clergyman who was most attentive and very good company. I was rather amused as we thought he was interested in my mother. I think Mam was rather tickled too. It turned out that it was me he was interested in and this raised my rather low morale. I didn't have the sympathy then to wonder how it affected my mother.

Holidays began to loom rather large in my plans while I was at college. I went to Scarborough for three successive summers to earn money as a waitress. Being a student made the job socially acceptable, I met different sorts of people and the tips made it worthwhile. Then in September I went off to Denmark or Austria or western Europe or Scotland. So the summers were very pleasant and the waitressing light and relaxing.

Three years passed. I'd gone in at seventeen as an immature schoolgirl and I'd become a hard working graduate at twenty, who was totally self-taught. The History we were examined on was British and European from about 410 A.D. to about 1900. This was called Modern History, in contrast to Ancient History, but I had had to answer only one question after 1700 as my interests had lain in the earlier periods. People couldn't understand why I knew nothing about the nineteenth and twentieth centuries.

That all had to be learned later when I became a teacher.

CHAPTER FIVE

A CONSTANT PERFORMANCE

There never was any question of going away to college as, although my mother was ambitious for me, her experience was limited. I qualified as a teacher at twenty-one and immediately began applying for jobs away from home. I was appointed to teach History and Latin at Harrogate College and left happily to live in.

All the buildings were on Duchy of Lancaster land and were of a pleasing grey stone. The gardens were still a mass of flowers and each day I enjoyed the six minute walk from Swinton House to School. The girls of York and Lancaster Houses had to run round the rather large block as they lived in main school so that they got some fresh air before lessons, but all the others just walked over. As a Teacher entered the playground two or three girls would rush to carry her books. This training in pleasant small talk and self-confidence was a good idea for the girls, but could be quite a burden for the teacher. Every single journey you braced yourself to face a stream of polite inquiries about your health or the weather.

It was amazing to be on the other side of school life. I liked being called Miss Kirkley and having doors opened for me. I thought Staff Meetings were most interesting and loved checking the girls' clothes on their first day. Staff had a special place to sit in chapel and in the hall and each classroom had a teacher's desk on a dais. There was as much to learn as when I'd started my own secondary school. Perhaps more as there was no hiding as one of a crowd now.

What I hadn't expected was the sheer volume of work. I had worked hard at University, but there were few deadlines and no basic problems about coping with the requirements of a History degree. As a teacher I had deadlines roughly every forty minutes and each lesson had to be thoroughly prepared. The girls had one textbook and there was nothing else to hand out or give them. The library was small and out of date, while the duplicating you had to do yourself on an old fordigraph. I had major problems finding materials for myself, never mind the girls. At college, I had discussed the effect of the new Protestant Churches on the political and economic structure of Europe, but I couldn't tell the story of Martin Luther in a way calculated to interest girls of thirteen or fourteen. I'd read huge chunks from Mein Kampf, but couldn't explain why the German people voted Hitler into power.

Not only was the preparation a never ending burden, as I taught from Year Eight to Year Thirteen, but I had an O Level, a repeat O Level and an A Level class. I knew that I was on trial in an exam as well as the pupils. I knew hardly any history after 1750, yet all the examinations were on later periods so I was reading for my own information as well as planning how to teach them. My own interests had been the Anglo Saxons and early Normans, yet the syllabus whisked through them in two or three lessons.

On top of this came something that I had never expected to be such a burden. The marking!

If you've never taught you can have no conception of the magnitude of this burden. Thirty essays on Bismarck, each three sides in length, to be read and corrected at ten at night will take intense concentration until midnight. Even with excellent planning you cannot get through the week with one piece of marking a day as there are perhaps eight separate classes all needing their work marked. And mark I had to. You could get away with the odd test but every fortnight there was the public reading of the whole class's marks.

Each subject teacher had to put down a mark out of ten for each girl in each of her classes; a mark that had to be substantiated with written evidence. The resulting ten or twelve for every person was then averaged and the averages for everyone placed in rank order. The Headmistress came round and read out the list in order of merit and commented where she thought it appropriate.

Not only was the humiliation very public for those at the bottom of the list, but you risked relegation unless you could get higher. Occasionally, girls even disappeared altogether from the bottom of the lower class, but this was rare, for it would have been an admission that the entrance examination had totally failed to select those who would benefit from an academic education.

Not only did I spend several hours a day marking work, but it took time to do all this collating of marks, averaging and creating an order of merit. If every teacher had filled in her marks you were lucky and could get the job done in under an hour. It was terribly important to get the arithmetic right as a slight slip could have such serious consequences.

It took me two years of extremely hard work to learn enough history to be confident of my material. The workload blotted out all leisure in term time and the weekly duties were just an interruption to preparation. I'd never valued sport or been much use at it, so I was certainly not in sympathy with the daily physical activities of the girls. They had at least an hour and a half of Games every day except Sunday. This of course, was the slavish imitation of Boys Schools and it was heresy to suggest that time might be better spent reading or with a hobby. Even the suggestion of different games was unacceptable. Netball, lacrosse, cricket and rounders followed each other inexorably throughout the year.

The duties were a real burden when you had so much work to do. At least one afternoon with games and one evening till ten. There wasn't a lot to do in the evening except be on call and ring the various bedtime bells but you couldn't settle down to work or you'd overrun the bell time. Then there were weekend duties. There was a half-day either Saturday or Sunday for two weekends out of three, so you rarely had a whole day to yourself except every third weekend. I took to going home then to get out of the claustrophobic atmosphere. Home didn't seem so bad: I could go out or sit in silence and I didn't feel I had to work all the time.

We didn't get paid for these duties. Who would put up with this exploitation nowadays? That part of our salary which was deducted for our residence was income tax free. We got nothing else. So the Government paid a small amount towards our salary in this way and the school, which was owned by an Insurance Company, got free but highly qualified labour.

There were a few teachers who lived out in the town and we regarded them as amazingly normal. People with flats or even whole houses, who could entertain and have a social life. The resident staff were either young like me who didn't know what they were coming to, or elderly impoverished women with no other home. The two groups rubbed along up to a point but had nothing in common.

Coming as I did straight from the intense social and intellectual life of a University, the contrast was almost overwhelming. I could get no-one to go to a dance with me so did what was almost unheard of in those days, I went alone. I met a nice boy who was very doubtful of such conduct, but who hung around for a few weeks, till the summer holiday put a natural end to a very slight relationship. I felt I was immured in a convent and felt very resentful. If there were presentable single men in Harrogate I certainly never met them.

Somehow that seemed to be my fault and everyone was rather patronising about what seemed an almost unmentionable interest.

What saved me in every way was the fact that I discovered I loved teaching. To me it was a performance I gave seven or eight times a day. The audience was by no means a captive one and I had some problems of control, but only in the first year and only with one or two classes. If I could get silence I could start the story telling that was my basic technique. Once I had the class's interest I could question and challenge and make the girls think. I was young, quite pretty, painted my fingernails and had one or two charming outfits and this, combined with a moderately heretical approach to a few sacred cows, ensured popularity.

One day the Senior Mistress drew me to one side and in a rather embarrassed way asked if I could try to fit in more with the type of clothes worn by the older staff. "Have you noticed that we also wear a sort of uniform? The Head would appreciate it if you wouldn't wear nail varnish, for example. I've noticed that the girls look to see what shoes you are wearing in the evening and that is rather undesirable. Sensible stockings and tweed skirts are what most of us prefer."

I was so amazed at anyone thinking the older staff worth copying and so hurt that anyone should take exception to my two modest dresses and three or four skirts, that I was totally silenced. I wasn't too secure to start with and it took me a long time to pick myself up off the floor. Later, I told her that I wouldn't do what she asked and she just smiled pleasantly and walked away. Such was the exchange of ideas at Harrogate.

The girls thought some of my ideas way out too. I had the whole Lower Sixth on Friday Evening for Current Affairs. About fifty girls were crammed into one room at a time when everyone thought they'd done enough work for the week. In 1952 I commented that travel to the moon would come in our lifetime and I can still remember the howl of derision that nearly lifted the roof off. Their lives were very sheltered and they expected all nice people to be Conservatives. I made them learn about all the major parties, which they enjoyed, but it caused one of the Music teachers to believe me a communist. For the last year she would neither meet my eye nor talk to me and certainly believed people like me were the downfall of the country.

There were about six full-time music teachers and two full-time diction and drama teachers. As two of us covered the whole school in History, and there was initially only one person for Geography, this gives some idea of how the school had developed. No wonder people still referred to it as Harrogate Ladies College. Everyone did Latin in those days and I had to teach it to twelve year-olds. I had always hated it both at school and college so tried to get a bit of fun into the lessons, but that was easier said than done. There was no Cookery of course and though there must have been Art, I certainly never saw any work on display.

Each week girls had to learn the Collect and they weren't free until it was mastered. I doubt if they all understood it but hopefully the beautiful language stood them in good stead. Each Wednesday after lunch there was a spelling test and about twenty words were tested from the school's own book. I used to give them seventeen spellings and three meanings which they thought most unfair, but I argued that being able to spell a word you didn't use or understand was profitless.

The girls were nearly all lovely. They were a joy to teach and were most appreciative of anything you did to make their lives cheerful. They were generally happy and got on well together but spent a lot of time wishing it was the end of term or an exeat. They lived in Houses of about forty-five and their ages ranged from twelve to eighteen. There was a pleasant atmosphere and very firm friendships were formed within the Houses. I belonged to Swinton House, the newest, and also felt more warmly towards the Swinton girls.

Each house had a House mistress, a matron and a handyman. Our handyman was Johnson who had served at Dunkirk and been part of the force holding the retreat. When the evacuation was complete they were ordered to surrender and Johnson spent the next five years as a prisoner of war in Germany. He had been wounded and received only minimal medical care, so the pieces of shrapnel still in his body used to surface periodically. He disappeared for spells in hospital. This was rather inconvenient, but Miss Wilson, our House mistress, wouldn't hear of having him replaced. She had had a senior position in the WAAF during the war and wasn't going to allow Johnson further suffering. Both of them told tales of wartime experiences and this was marvellous for me as I was teaching about the Second World War and needed all the information I could get. Strangely, I knew few people who had fought in the war. My uncle had been in the army but he never got further than Gibraltar and never saw action. My father had fought in the First World War and lived through a great deal of action, so I felt I could hold my head up when talking to Johnson, but couldn't contribute in any first-hand way.

Miss Wilson taught P.E. and Games which was quite an achievement as she must have been in her fifties. She never complained but I think she must have been often bone weary. She had known both Douglas Bader and Leonard Cheshire and after them, I must have been very small beer. Her biggest problem, however, was Matron.

In the three years I was at Harrogate and living in the same house as Mrs Davidson, Swinton's Matron, I never had a pleasant word from her. I don't know whether she objected to teachers in general or me in particular. Probably all teachers! She had a dog which was her pride and joy and which certainly got more attention than any girl. One Saturday lunch time six of the young staff had made a lunch in Swinton kitchen. The kitchen was rarely used and as we were all sick of communal dining we planned a meal of soup, cold meats and salad. The only cooking we did was the soup and the final coffee. We had just finished and were enjoying the sense of liberation the small treat had given us when Mrs Davidson burst in like a thunderbolt. She roared and yelled and stood in the kitchen blazing with anger. Her final condemnation, spat at us with a mixture of contempt and derision was, "And you've used the dog's pans."

Stunned and crushed we began the washing up, the whole day spoiled. What inadequacies or megalomania could have caused the woman to spew out such hatred I cannot imagine but it was a display of passion I have never forgotten. No staff ever again visited us in

Swinton; we always had to go to their Houses.

The girls didn't see this side of Mrs. Davidson and I'm sure she kept their socks and blouses in apple-pie order. Each girl had three dressing table drawers and half a wardrobe and it was a crush to get everything in. Six pairs of knickers, six pairs of knicker linings, six blouses, one woollen dress with detachable collars for wearing after tea during the week, one silk dress also in green with detachable collars for wear on warm Sundays, one suit, one overcoat and, most beloved of all, the floor-length, green cloak which was tossed on when running between House and School. This lasted a girl her whole school career. The uniform was extensive and expensive and in 1955 cost well over two hundred pounds. This was slightly less than half my annual salary. Girls also thought the clothes were very expensive, especially when a whole term passed on one occasion without them wearing their silk Triks. They knew their parents were doing their best to give them a good education, often at considerable sacrifice. No-one thought that an expensive uniform, fitted at Jenners of Edinburgh, contributed very much.

Harrogate was the first school I had ever been in that had carpets on many floors and good furniture. There were often bowls of flowers too which created a civilised atmosphere. The Headmistress, Miss Todd, took prayers every day in the chapel and once a week she gave out notices in the hall, but she never talked to the school about anything other than administration. After her daily sortie she was never seen again by the girls except at the dreaded mark reading. No personality came across and as a role model she was useless. I cannot imagine anyone wanting to be like her. Yet she must have been efficient as the school expanded during her time and there was always a waiting list.

Staff saw her one additional time each week at the Staff Meeting. This was a half-hour period when she rehearsed what she would say to a visiting Parent. As she never spoke to any girl except in the public mark reading, she had to ask her teachers what to say. Whole terms passed without me even teaching one of the girls under discussion and that half-hour became a time in limbo. You could neither work nor talk; you just endured. Between forty and fifty of us were subjected to this total waste of time each week and I do not remember any general discussion whatsoever. However, I think she knew who I was. I was the one in high heels, lipstick and nail varnish.

The only thing I liked about her was her birthday. Not particularly the fact that she had been born, but the annual celebration. If the weather was fine the whole school went out for the day. This was the one of only two breaks from routine that we ever had, the other being an epidemic. The irritating thing was that it was always a secret until we were actually mounting the coaches. You worked flat out the night before preparing lessons and getting the books marked only to find the school a whirling cauldron of rumour before breakfast. Girls and Junior Staff were never told anything but the Establishment seemed to have overlooked the fact that even an efficient kitchen cannot produce four hundred packed lunches without some extra activity. Activity which bored girls were quick to note.

The outings were to beautiful spots in Yorkshire. Had the History and Geography staff known in advance we might not have been caught in states of ignorance about Fountains and Bolton Abbey and the lovely river valleys we walked along. Three hundred and fifty girls in bottle green suits and overcoats all walking, never running or playing, making conversation with the teacher in charge of their group. The teacher, if it was me, could be wearing rather unsuitable shoes. Each year I faced the same dilemma. If I listened to the rumour and went back to change my shoes I risked spending the whole day in flat shoes. This was no problem if the rumour turned out to be true but the large number of false alarms meant a sizeable risk. And it was a real risk. It was to be five and a half years before I dared teach a lesson in flat shoes.

The reason for secrecy was to avoid the mass hysteria which would have resulted had bad weather caused cancellation. The whole school would then have been uncontrollable. Normally the school was calm and routine dulled us all. It was an inward looking world and the Cold War, Suez or Oil Crises caused no ripple. Girls were to be protected from disease too and staff were asked not to go into Woolworths or Marks and Spencers in case we brought infection back. Obviously, there was a social hierarchy among germs. Certain flu germs hadn't understood this and invaded the College one winter. Nearly everyone except Swinton Matron and I, went down with a high temperature and had about five days in bed. The treatment was simple. You had your temperature taken. If it was 99.5 or higher you went to bed and starved. If it was between 99 and 99.5 you were allowed up and had slushy porridge-like meals. When it was normal you went back to school.

There were three weeks of total chaos. Girls and teachers fell ill in illogical groupings and the relays of sick, not yet sick and recovering but irritable, coincided with no school structure. Classes were put together and were taught anything that came to the mind of the teacher suddenly put in charge. She was herself sickening or convalescent and couldn't have cared less about what girls got up to as long as it was quiet. Even the Music Teachers were put in charge of classes and their complaints revealed what every one had guessed: that they couldn't do much else than play the piano. I tottered around believing that I was saving the world; teaching ten lessons a day, taking temperatures, carrying enormous loads of food to several houses, visiting the sick, and even managing a civil exchange with Matron who, irritatingly, didn't get the flu either.

Three years passed. I'd learned to teach, keep order, ignore the Head and I was comfortable with Gladstone, Disraeli, Rommel and Churchill. I'd learned a lot of history and how not to run a school. The younger girls, who were twelve to thirteen had roughly ten minutes a day free time and I thought this criminal. Every moment was accounted for until eight pm. Then they had till eight-ten pm to do what they wanted in their common room before the bedtime bell. Lights out for them was at eight-thirty-five pm and they were certainly dead tired. So much time was wasted going back and forth and changing their clothes while each meal, eaten formally in the Dining Hall, took an age. The food was nourishing, plain stuff and a new cook who made trifles and gave them sliced lambs hearts in sauce was asked to leave after one term. Towards the very end of term the food improved noticeably so that parents who took their daughters' complaints seriously, lost sympathy when they heard of roast pork with baked potatoes, peas and carrots followed by spotted dick and custard on Monday followed by liver, bacon, cabbage, onions and tinned pears and custard on Tuesday.

In fact the kitchen staff were at the heart of the whole institution. There was a cooked breakfast at eight, full lunch at one, tea at four and dinner at seven-thirty. And three hundred and fifty girls and about twenty-five staff sat down in one place while another twenty-five staff sat down in two small dining rooms elsewhere. And this was seven days a week. I don't know how the shifts were organised yet, though domestic staff were difficult to get, I never remember late meals or any sort of disaster. It was just that meals were slow and immovable. I would have preferred the educational side to be pivotal.

Florence was the doyenne of all the kitchen maids. She'd been at the College for about thirty years and it was her pride and joy to lead in the Christmas procession with the boar's head. Dark brown, glazed, with the traditional orange in its mouth, it was borne on a silver salver the length of the hall to the accompaniment of tremendous cheers. Gorgeous aromas trailing behind turned us all into Bisto Kids and merged with those of the roast turkey, the pyramids of mince pies and the huge Christmas Pudding. There were baskets of fruit wrapped in gold and silver foil and at the end of this procession came the Wassail cup. We couldn't all drink from the Wassail Cup, huge though it was, so every silver sporting trophy the school owned had been polished till it shone, filled with fruit cup and was passed round while those not actually drinking at the moment sang the Wassailing song at the tops of their voices.

Exhausted with cheering and good will we all then went to eat a splendid Christmas dinner to regain our strength. Back in the hall an hour later, we sat in candle light singing carols until Father Christmas arrived with bells and music and laughter and bright lights. The pile of presents was huge and gloriously wrapped and cheers greeted the name of each lucky recipient. We all knew that each girl received a gift once in her school career, so no-one minded much if it was this year or next.

Then over to the Chapel for stillness, the old story of the Birth of a Saviour and a blessing before each House went carolling back in a torch light procession.

The next day we all went home.

CHAPTER SIX

FRAGRANT HARBOUR

I was born on a Thursday but I don't think that that alone made me want to work in a glamorous place like Hong Kong.

After two schools, each totally different, I realized that work didn't vary very much and something exciting was needed to make the thought of the next thirty years bearable. A Thai friend thought that Hong Kong had a climate more suitable for Europeans so, being a fan of the writer Pearl Buck, I set my heart on that. Hong Kong was the nearest I got to China until 1984 but I had four wonderful years there and it remains a watershed in my life.

The first problem was to get a job. For a long time I watched the foreign section of the Times Educational Supplement but no-one wanted a History teacher anywhere in the Far East. A temporary teacher came to the Newcastle school where I was and I was delighted to find that she was on leave from an Anglican School in Hong Kong. Although she told me lots about Hong Kong and her school, there was no chance of a post there as the two Historians were set for the next decade or two. It did sound such a good school though and life in Hong Kong seemed wonderful.

The miracle happened. The only History post to be advertised for the whole of Hong Kong appeared in the TES. It was for St. Stephens, Miss Corney's school. I couldn't believe it. Miss Corney couldn't believe it either and exercised her mind continuously on whose post it was. But the vacancy was genuine and I did get it and life revved up again. The teacher, who had left so unexpectedly was Joyce Bennet, who eventually became the second Anglican woman priest, and she had gone to do more Church work. I trust everyone benefited as much as me from that vocation.

There certainly were aeroplanes in those days but everyone seemed to go out by sea. I duly embarked at Liverpool on a cargo ship, The Laocoon, waved off by my parents and aunt. I didn't feel guilty even though my brother had just left home too and my mother was feeling rather depressed and useless. They stood on the quay waving for over an hour and I was glad when eventually a bend hid them from sight. This was not so much because farewells were a strain but because we had slowed down and eventually stopped altogether. Engine failure at the beginning of an eight thousand mile journey sapped every-one's confidence but mine; nothing could touch my optimism. After nearly a day's delay we eventually got going again and I gave only a flitting thought to the naming of the ship. Neither engine failure nor sea serpents would stop me.

The eight passengers were immediately given tea and cakes as a distraction and thus began a marathon eating programme. The meals were enormous. Each meal had its menu but you could have everything on it. No need to select. The only limitation was that you had really to be finished in half-an-hour. I was at the Chief Engineer's table and that was the time he allocated to his social responsibilities. The Captain's table ate more leisurely, so those who sat there could sample a greater range of courses.

The speed of meals was a disappointment as we had absolutely nothing else to do all day. There was scrabble in the evening; every evening. After forty-two consecutive evenings playing scrabble I vowed I would never play the game again and that is a vow I have kept. During the morning we had a sweepstake on yesterday's mileage and this was a five minute excitement. Of the eight passengers two were children so did not participate. The law of averages would indicate that each of the six of us would win seven times, but as a good Methodist I had reservations about this irresponsible use of money and though I joined in daily, I never once won. I became the wonder of all and during the last week I trembled that things would change. They didn't and I left feeling that my half-baked principle had triumphed without inconveniencing me.

We none of us could take any real exercise. At the beginning we had taken short but brisk walks to the bows or skipped round the deck but that soon had to stop. There were two racehorses stabled on the foredeck in stout timber structures and we had only had two or three days at sea before they became angry and fretful at the total lack of exercise. After a week they became dangerous and we were banned from going near them. Only one sailor ever approached them and he was tolerated only as the bringer of food and the mucker out. Some one must have had more money than sense as their condition deteriorated drastically and though both were delivered alive, one certainly had to be put down on arrival. The accompaniment to the whole voyage was the thump, thump, thump of the non-stop kicking and our world shrank even further till it embraced the saloon, the cabin, the bath room and two narrow strips of deck along each side.

Suez, Aden, Port Sweetenham and Singapore were our stops. The longest was for ten days at Port Sweetenham where we exchanged the tedium of the ship for the tedium of the Missions to Seamen. The ship was our whole world and I became very inward looking, bored on board but frightened of leaving.

Hong Kong was incredibly beautiful as I woke up to it one morning. I didn't have time to be scared as three of my new colleagues were there to meet me.

A new life had certainly begun.

I never tired of the beauty of Hong Kong. I thought I might stop noticing it after a while but that never did happen. The combination of mountains and sea, the colours of both and the constant life meant it was always fascinating. St. Stephens was in an old colonial building half-way up the mountain slope and we sat at the dining room table looking out at one of the great views of the world. The Japanese had used it as a hospital during the occupation but the Diocese had initially built it as a school for Chinese girls and it looked as if it could last for ever.

Each of the Resident Staff had a room which was probably higher than it was long and mine was filled with enormous blackwood furniture. There were two modern bathrooms but there were also several Chinese baths: huge pots into which you clambered, looking like the missionary being cooked for the cannibals' dinner. The four floors were built round a courtyard and the height of the rooms made it quite high. Not high as buildings are high today in Hong Kong, but high enough to be terrifying when builders put up, or worse, threw down the bamboo scaffolding. The enormous poles were literally thrown down and caught four floors below by one man wearing gloves.

St Stephens had a garden which seemed a miracle even in those early days. When we were on duty we took the Boarders on their daily walk through this garden and along to the University garden. There was so little open space in the colony that this was a rare privilege: I knew that, but in those days I had no interest in any plant or tree, so missed all sorts of interesting things. I was amazed how green Hong Kong was. I'd seen too many films of parched tropical earth and had expected the same.

I had no map. People pointed out this island and that island and talked familiarly of Castle Peak and Shek O, yet it never occurred to me to buy a map and there were no orientation diagrams to help tourists. The only person I knew with a map was the Geography teacher and when she lent it to me, it was a revelation. My generation mustn't have been map conscious as hardly any of us had maps when we visited any big Far Eastern city. I only remember two shops which stocked English books and I never saw any maps on display. There were parts of Hong Kong I never placed until I was back in England.

As I took trams and buses around the city I saw the crowded, colourful streets with high dwellings crammed together. Neon lighting was everywhere and blazed out in the evening in reds and yellows and orange. Sometimes the road was so near a dwelling that you could see a room packed with three story wooden bunks, each one of which was someone's total private space. At least the ones I could see were rented out for twenty-four hours at a time. There were similar bunk spaces which could be hired for eight hours and shifts of sleepers went in and out. I had been much moved by a display of refugee conditions in the Churchyard of St Martin's in the Fields, a year or two earlier in England and I now saw similar shanty dwellings frequently.

This dire poverty was always there. There was no escape from an awareness of tragedy and need. The seemingly prosperous, middle-class, fee-paying St Stephen's had its share of despair. In my first month a student admitted to member of staff that the bailiffs were in their one room flat, along with the family and the body of her dead father. They would not release him for burial until the debt had been paid. It was such a small debt to cause such desperation, such an horrific form of blackmail, and it was so easily solved by a few people giving something from their surplus.

There were hardly any beggars. There were places where free meals were provided but most people tried to manage and find work. The Churches all did an enormous amount of social work and helped to educate, heal and feed the unfortunate. The Hong Kong Jockey

Club gave enormous sums to a great range of Charities and this helped me to drop my half-baked disapproval of gambling as well as being so valuable to the unfortunate. I was anxious to do my bit, so volunteered to help in a Clinic but after a few weeks I had to acknowledge that I was no earthly use and would be far better helping people to get qualifications: to help in a more informed way.

The streets below the school were an old part of the city; the pavements were colonnaded and the shops set back. Most of the columns had a rat box attached and the one I looked in was certainly being put to its intended purpose. Many shops were packed with gold and jade. Brilliant lighting blazed over coins and rings, bracelets and necklaces, earrings and medallions. Each of the hundreds of shops had at least one customer. The customer might look too poor to afford a meal or he might arrive in a sleek, black limousine with lace curtains to preserve anonymity, but both were taken seriously and the negotiations for a good price went on for some time.

Above were the rooms and flats of the middle-class, the tradesmen and the craftsmen. In this part of town I was usually the only European and was totally ignored. I could watch the ivory carvers sitting in their tiny kiosks and the chop makers; I could see the letter writers being consulted by their customers and the barber with his chair, cut-throat razor and mirror tucked into a back lane. Here I saw pornography displayed for the first time and bootblacks sitting on their hunkers on the kerb. There were food shops and restaurants and market stalls and children carrying the bamboo baskets that the dumplings and spring rolls and vegetables had been steamed in. Everyone seemed to be busy and, though people did talk to each other in the street, there were few people just chatting.

Overhead were signs to indicate Doctors and Dentists and Acupuncturists and fortune tellers. There was the shop that sold the furniture and money for the dead next door to the workshop selling superb coffins. The money that was burned for the departed after the funeral was printed in English as well as Chinese and the colossal sums were drawn on the Bank of Hell in Hong Kong currency. Every small lane running into the main road had its stalls of handbags and sweaters and children's clothes and underwear and fabrics. The fabrics were a constant wonder and all women haunted these stalls to buy the cloth that one of the thousands of tailors would make up for you. There was every fabric you could want, from plain cotton and wool to silk brocades and embroidered gauze that would not have looked out of place in the Forbidden City. Chinese, European and Indian tastes had to be catered for and the choice was overwhelming.

Western chemist shops sparkled and gleamed with light and cleanliness while in the next block Chinese medicine shops were dark and secretive. Large jars and bowls held the insides of every imaginable animal and reptile while bunches of herbs and weirdly shaped ginseng roots were stacked in baskets; the raw material of the remedies made up individually for each customer.

There was a House of Rest where the dead lay until the funeral and all friends visited to mourn loudly and, further along, a Temple which had a constant stream of people burning joss sticks and standing for a moment or two before the altar. It was a noisy, busy place, remarkably dirty and the only single story building in the whole of that suburb. Outside were the only dropouts I was aware of in the colony: a European and a couple of Chinese men who lay on the only benches to be found in hundreds of miles of streets.

Many of our students would come from the two or three-roomed tiny flats in this or similar neighbourhoods. Often they had long journeys in the packed trams and buses though sometimes a group would squeeze into their regular hired car. Others were from extremely rich families and came by chauffeur-driven car. I had barely been in the colony a week when the whole Resident Staff were invited out to lunch at the home of one of them. There seemed no question of anyone not going as the Head had accepted for us all, so about a dozen of us left for the Woo mansion.

It was the first Chinese house I had been in and I knew how lucky I was. Lots of Europeans never get inside a Chinese house at all. It had a garden which was amazing and it used the traditional trees, stones and water. It also had a mini zoo and I was very much taken aback to find a shallow pit of live snakes next to a group of penned cranes. The cranes were in constant distress but no-one seemed concerned but me. It's to be hoped that the family ate the snakes fairly soon.

Inside the large main salon was like a museum. Actually it was a museum. Enormous blackwood cases reached from floor to ceiling, not just round the walls but jutting out at right angles too, forming perhaps six or seven alcoves. In each alcove display tables took up much of the area so that, although it was a huge room, there was actually very little space to sit. Every case, every table and every flat surface was full of blue and white china. Not just a range of different objects but all enormous plates and bowls. I believe much of it was Ming and certainly all of it was valuable but I couldn't get over the fact that this was the main reception room of a rich family but it was the most unhome-like place I could imagine and quite uncomfortable. I wish now I had had the confidence to ask for some instruction in appreciating the china, but Mr Woo rather waved away an early tentative inquiry. It may have been an investment rather than a much loved hobby.

We all sat round a circular table for lunch so my first attempt with chopsticks was very public. I seem to remember liking everything and finding it recognisable until we came to that delicacy, sharks fin soup. This was so slimy and glutinous that I had great difficulty in getting it down and it was to take many feasts before I grew to like it. I liked it so much eventually that I ignored the uneasy awareness that the fins were gained at the cost of appalling injuries to the fisher people of the South East Asian Islands.

Mr Woo was only in Hong Kong for a few weeks, though his wife and daughter lived there all the time. He actually lived in Shanghai where I expect he had another wife and family. Pearl Buck had prepared me for this but what I found amazing was the fact that he still owned and ran and took the profit from his factory in Shanghai. He had an even larger house there and had as many if not more servants. And this, in a Communist country where I had thought private property strictly limited

Although I was treated, along with the others, with the greatest courtesy, I felt it had been an opportunity for Mr Woo to gain face. I couldn't really accept that he wanted to meet twelve Western women for their own sake and the fact that he spent most of the time telling us things or questioning the Head, rather supported this view. Certainly Beatrice, our student, gained face among her classmates and I had had my first glimpse inside a Chinese house.

Teaching began again. The colony might be magic but the daily slog of preparation, teaching and marking never stopped. One problem I had not envisaged was the lack of information. The school library was tiny and geared more for the youngsters than the staff while the only Library in the colony was the small British Council Library which had little history in it. This was a huge problem when I came to teach the Far Eastern sections of both the O and A Level syllabuses. As I had no Chinese or Japanese I had no original sources at all and was dependent on what had been published in America. There was hardly anything from Britain. I also had to buy these books from the tiny stock held by the booksellers. I have always appreciated a good Lending Library since then.

I was most uneasy about the material I was teaching the students. It had to be done in English for the Public Exam but they already knew it all as they had lessons in Chinese history from Miss Dai. Sadly Miss Dai and I could not communicate in each other's languages so I could not learn from her. The students were no help as they had had so much respect for scholars, a category in which I was graciously included, that they could not reveal my mistakes. Years later the supposed firsthand accounts of Sir Edmund Backhouse about the Dowager Empress Tsu Hsi were revealed as a pack of lies but it was even longer before I read her Biography by Seagrave which presented a totally different picture of her and gave a rational account of parties struggling for power in Beijing. It is always difficult to teach a class that knows more than you do and humbling to realize that they didn't agree with you, but say nothing.

At least the girls didn't know much Japanese history. I was happier with that but the Chinese attitude to the Japanese was ambivalent. On the one hand they were pleased that they owed so much to China, but on the other, jealous that they had modernized themselves so successfully. There had been nearly ten years of war between them and an occupation of Hong Kong that their families could remember, so warmth was lacking.

This inability to get information was difficult for Europeans. There were a couple of daily papers in English but they were very subservient to Government. Some Chinese papers took a more independent line but access was difficult and no Chinese person seemed willing to challenge what were sometimes quite balmy ideas. For several months the English language papers supported the unification of Malaya, Singapore and a bit of Borneo on the principle that they were racially the same. We were expected to

68

swallow a political expedient masquerading as a liberal reform and no-one was surprised when the Federation fell apart and Singapore soared off into prosperity alone.

There were cultural differences which made my job harder. There was the tradition of respect for older people and for scholars and the tradition of respect for the official line. This came to a head with each group of students each year over the topic of the First Chinese War - the Opium War - in 1839. What arrogance that I don't even know what the Chinese called it. The war was caused by the wilful importing of Indian Opium into China despite its horrendous moral, medical and economic consequences and despite the Beijing Government's undoubted right to legislate against it. Yet no pupil criticised the British merchants or the British Government that sent gun boats to support the infamous trade or the fact that one of the consequences was the ceding of territory from a sovereign state.

Indeed, so anxious were the students to avoid offence that the next essay to come in was an account of Chinese weaknesses and errors which practically made the war their own fault.

This saying the pleasant thing instead of the truthful thing was a most difficult thing to contend with. If I persuaded a few students to pursue intellectually honest thoughts, use evidence to reach conclusions and to challenge ideas that were false, then my time in the colony was more than the self-indulgence I often thought it. Probably the passivity was one of the consequences of a patriarchal government as well as a cultural unwillingness to assert individualism.

The girls all worked very hard. Each year the entrance exam selected sixty from about three hundred applicants who had already passed the Primary Six, or Twelve Plus Exam. This was a harrowing day as all the twelve year-olds turned up in new clothes and new hairdos. What exam could select fairly from such a large group? However a selection was made and the successful ones came in September, in the uniform cheongsam, full of hope and excitement. Often the hopes of the whole extended family rested on their young shoulders and a successful student would drag her whole family up the ladder as she eventually qualified for teaching or medicine or banking.

It was the only school where I've told students not to work so hard. "Take a break this weekend." "Go out somewhere tonight and forget about work." "Try to come back refreshed". I doubt if they did. Of course, when the students worked so hard, the teachers could do no less so the marking was heavier than ever. No-one, but no-one, ever failed to do their homework. I hardly remember anyone ever being absent. Even the girl whose house had been caught in a landslide during a typhoon turned up as soon as the all clear was given, despite the fact that her younger brother was buried within. She came all during the next two or three days as the relief workers tried to reach him and she never did have time off as there was no funeral. At least it was warm and safe in St. Stephens.

Hong Kong was a place where most of us worked hard and played hard. There were night clubs and bars and the best shopping in the world. There was every imaginable restaurant and the lovely smells of street kitchens grilling, stir frying and simmering delicious soups. Of course Miss Corney warned me against eating anything from the street and memories of those in earlier generations, who had died from typhoid or cholera or dysentery, was firmly fixed in all our minds after we had visited the European cemetery in Macau and seen how short a life some people had had in the East. We even ate imported lettuce.

There was considerable social life connected with the Churches and with the army which had its polo matches and go-cart racing. There was a race course in Happy Valley but I didn't discover the joys of racing until much later. There were clubs and meetings but no politics. I spent hours in a Drama Group, loving the performances and the intimacy of the intense six week rehearsal period. The standard was very high for amateur drama and we did some adventurous plays which the public sometimes liked and sometimes didn't. The Governor and his wife came to the "Resounding Tinkle" and were believed to be unable to make anything of it yet some of the audience were helpless with laughter.

Walking was rather difficult and so was getting away on your own. If you had a boat or hired a launch you could find a deserted beach, but the fact that you were there attracted others, who came and sat down right beside you. Still, the swimming was good and the sunshine was so reliable that it was possible to arrange a barbecue or a sunrise party well ahead and be pretty sure it would happen.

There was golf and squash and sailing for those who wanted it and far more invitations to people's houses than I'd ever known before. Entertaining becomes effortless when you have plenty of servants. My first Christmas in Hong Kong was marked by indigestion as I was invited to three different houses during the two days and then we ourselves had a huge party with Christmas dinner in the evening of St Stephen's Day (Boxing Day). Four Christmas Dinners in thirty two hours: one lived at full stretch all the time.

Chinese friends played mahjong, went to banquets and spent a lot of time on the telephone. There seemed to be little interest in sport, either active or as a spectator, which was just as well as there were few facilities. At St Stephen's we had Health and Beauty each morning before lessons, a sort of mass bend and stretch session with the whole school together, but it took the constant authority of the Head to enforce it. Indeed, Miss Cherry had to go along herself to join in else the girls would have faded away.

I packed lots of living into my four years but my contract was finished. I had to decide whether to renew it or go home to England. It was a hard decision but there was no career future for me as a European and a Methodist in a Chinese community and an Anglican school. The friends I had at the end of the four years were totally different from those I had at the beginning. People came and went. Relationships were formed, blossomed and either wilted or ended in a remarkably brief time and you were forever saying good-bye as people went on leave or left. I didn't think that was a good basis for the rest of my life.

CHAPTER SEVEN

COMPREHENSION IN A COMPREHENSIVE SCHOOL

After a cosmopolitan four years in Hong Kong I wanted to live in London. Friends I'd made in school, church or drama club were not likely to come to the North of England, but they might come to the capital. It was a way of avoiding living back with my parents but London had always had the most tremendous glamour for me. It had had it when I took annual holidays with my Aunt and it was there for me still at thirty. I still think it's a wonderful city thirty years on. I was sure everyone else thought it marvellous too. Its parks, its museums, its great buildings and the names straight from history and literature are a constant delight to me. I had never talked much to people who didn't care about such things.

This changed with my new post as Head of History in a large London Comprehensive. I thought I had had experience of slower learners in a previous school, so with a reasonable amount of confidence I embarked on a timetable which included teaching forms 2J and 4M. There were thirteen classes or streams lettered from A-N in most years and even the dumbest in M and N knew they were at the very bottom of the pile. Who graded these children at eleven, and on what grounds was a mystery to those who had to teach them. It was a devastation to those so labelled and such youngsters immediately learned to write themselves off. Often they were gentle kindly girls who tried their best to please their teachers, but a few were resentful at their low rating. Everyone's self confidence was so crushed that they thought there was little point in trying. A few were angry in a general, inarticulate way and this number grew as they got older.

Such classes, most with about thirty girls, were almost impossible to teach. Most were indeed very limited in ability. No way could you get round to see everyone's work: indeed, some needed so much help to start or needed everything explained twice that you didn't get round at all. In thirty-five minutes class and teacher reduced each other to quivering frustration. By the time the classes were aged fourteen and fifteen, the gentleness and kindness were noticeably less while the anger had grown. Very few staff could maintain even a semblance of order. Typing, English, Arithmetic and Cookery, girls could see the point of, but not much else.

"Why've we got to have an atlas?"

"To see where different countries are."

"Why? I'm not going anywhere."

"One day you might and anyway you hear about places on the News. It's nice to know where they are."

"What for? Who listens to the news anyway? I listen to Radio Caroline. That's the best and there's no news on that."

By the time you've quashed a lot of cross-class repartee about rival Radio Stations you get back to the atlas.

"Let's look at the West Indies on page so and so."

"I might go to the West Indies to see my gran one day."

Grab this opportunity quickly.

"Yes that would be lovely wouldn't it? You'd want to know where Jamaica was and which direction you'd be going in."

"No! Who cares? I'd get on a plane and get off in Jamaica. I don't need to know anything else."

She probably didn't either. Yet I'd grown up visiting a News Reel where we'd all spun a huge globe, stubbing a finger at Newcastle and gazing with awe at the distances across the States, Siberia and the Atlantic. I had to learn that there was no particular need to keep on acquiring information. I also had to learn that trying to impart information that others don't want is a waste of time. They don't want it for all sorts of reasons: it's boring, it's of no immediate utility or they know Society's low evaluation of themselves so in anger reject what society's representative, the teacher, is trying to do. Only if they really like you will they do their best. But with only seventy minutes a week there was no time to work at being liked.

". . . and so Marie Curie discovered Radium. What's Radium used for?"

Silence.

"Well, it's used in X-rays and can be used in curing cancer."

"You can't cure cancer." Emphatically.

"You can sometimes cure c. . . . . ."

"My Auntie died of cancer. You can't cure cancer."

"Oh, I'm sorry about that, but there are a few cancers that respond to . . . . ."

"You can't cure cancer." Even more emphatically.

"If you catch it early enough it may.. . . . ."

"You can't cure cancer. I know."

That was an argument I lost. I was shouted down. How could I have got a toe-hold in such a closed mind. I met arrogance, fury, contempt, bewilderment and silence. A few girls in these difficult classes never spoke; they'd learned to keep their heads down and avoid the confrontations that came in most lessons. If you are powerless you react either by keeping the lowest possible profile or by violence. Being a girls' school the violence was nearly all verbal. We had staff nervous breakdowns and resignations by the dozen. One year forty-three teachers left. Any system which crushes both pupils and teachers as this narrow streaming did, must be wrong. It must have been much the same in the Secondary Modern Schools which had the failed rejects of a whole system, certainly the bottom stream of a Grammar School was difficult to interest or control.

Thankfully, I was never to go back to it in later schools. There are ways of helping very backward girls keep their self-respect and willingness to learn, but telling them directly and indirectly for five years that they are stupid is not one of them.

I'd always taught in selective schools until then and enjoyed teaching clever pupils, but I'd been converted to the principle of the all ability secondary comprehensive school by Robin Pedley's book. Make no mistake there were very clever girls at this school too, and they did well and were a pleasure to teach. Society was telling them that they were really clever by putting them into the A or B Form for five years and making sure that they knew there were nearly three hundred girls of their own age beneath them. And they believed it.

I learned a lot about self fulfilling prophecies.

I'd thought I'd had a wide social background until this school but I'd always mixed with people, sometimes very poor or very uneducated people, who had valued education. They understood that bits of it could be trying but never doubted its overall value. Now I was meeting a whole section of people whose horizons were very limited. I began to understand what they didn't want. They didn't want patronage, useless information, challenging thoughts, jam tomorrow, being cooped up in school all day away from their real interests, homework, being told not to smoke or use bad language, going out for fire drill, having their parents lifestyle queried and especially, being reminded that without qualifications they'd not get a job. Of course they all got jobs. I was confusing literary skills with survival skills and most of them were better at the survival skills than I was.

The girls lived in South London and quite a few had been up West to shop, but little more. Each year we took Second Year classes to the Tower of London during the winter season and not one pupil seemed to have been there before. One girl admitted to never having been on a train before, so I had to learn that basic social education was an important part of my job. The Tower in winter in the 1960's was a cold, cheerless place with far fewer places open to visit than today and nowhere to eat our packed lunches. The Crown Jewels, which might have interested them, were not on our free tickets. Presumably some girls enjoyed themselves and glimpsed worlds and times beyond their own but a lot preferred to run up the four hundred plus stairs of the Monument and see the view from the top. We always started our tour by wearing off surplus energy in this way. We used to get tickets to Hampton Court too, but after several excursions where the only interest was raised by the Maze and the Great Vine, we gave them up.

Obviously the Capital, which delighted me even in winter had no such charms for many of my pupils. Books I had read as a child they didn't know and didn't want to know. This became an increasing problem for me as I realized that the sort of books they might enjoy simply were not available. They needed fairly sophisticated stories about working people and their families but in very simple language. They wanted discussion of issues like "nicking" things, living next to coloureds, getting and most important keeping a boyfriend, arranged marriages or setting yourself up as a hairdresser. Not Dickens. Only very slowly did such books come on the market in the 1970's. The history books we had were just as inadequate. So youngsters who had poor reading skills were further deprived by having little to enjoy. Learning to read is so very hard and takes so long, it's a pity if all you can then use it for are road signs and advertisements. Not only were resources inappropriate, but many of us teachers failed to realize what a revolution in learning had been caused by television. An enormous shift from literary to visual. The role models in Coronation Street or Crossroads rarely talked of anything but immediate personal concerns. Neither were they ever seen sitting reading books. Instead of using these programmes as teaching aids we were dismissive of them.

The abler classes and most of the Sixth Form were far easier to teach. The only disadvantage was the colossal amount of marking. If thirty girls write for thirty minutes as fast as they can on the causes of the Crimean War, or Disraeli's reforms or the effects of the coming of the railways; how many hours does it take to correct and assess each set? And if each of the four exam classes do this once a week you've got two-and-a-half hours of the most intense concentration - reading much the same thing thirty times. A minimum of ten hours a week. Then each A Level essay took twenty minutes to correct. The younger classes wrote less but it was even more boring while those who were in the J-N sets wrote like eight year-olds. Yet filling in the gaps and drawing weren't really the way to learn.

I had to accept that having some knowledge of your roots and society's development was less important to others than to me. Everyone was interested in life when their parents were young, but for many it had to be personalised, while some had no interest at all if the society wasn't recognisably like their own. What must it be like to hear all day about people and activities that were totally strange to you? This coincided with a time of rapidly increasing numbers of black pupils in the school and we were just beginning to use the term "culture shock". Some of my white pupils and I suffered from this too.

One serious consequence of this is loss of confidence and I felt it also. Not only did I seriously doubt my skills in my chosen career but the whole subject of History went through a period of crisis. Articles appeared in the Press challenging its value in the curriculum and all sorts of intelligent people dismissed it because it wasn't relevant. Everything had to be relevant. My personal life was overturned at the same time as I left my own flat one day at five minutes notice and never returned to live there. The high drama of a family crisis meant I went to live with my brother to look after his two children and there were some desperately unhappy times.

Things went from bad to worse at school too. There were good times and I made some good friends, had rewarding classes and started an ambitious programme of General Studies for the whole Sixth Form. There was a strong bond between the staff as we were united in our discomfort and our dislike of the Head. The discomfort was apparent when you realized there were only sixty-five chairs, no desks, no tables, three lavatories and no dining room for roughly a hundred and twenty women. There were about a dozen men on the staff and they had no toilets at all - until a whole set of girls' lavatories was given over to them. We weren't jealous of the generosity of their provision of what must have been one each, as they were up five flights of stairs. But the fact that we had nowhere to mark properly, only one very public phone and were perpetually queuing to use a lavatory lowered our own self-image.

The main disadvantage however, lay with the new Head who arrived after I'd been there six months. The atmosphere changed almost overnight from cheerful, relaxed but hard-working professionalism to a constant tense resentment. Never before had I properly understood the effect of Ship's Captains, Napoleons, Popes and other Absolute Monarchs on communities. I'd always thought in terms of economic forces, political pressures, changed objectives and underestimated the individual's dynamism.

Like an Early Stuart this Head knew she was always right. She had God totally on her side too and often reminded us that He had sent her to this school for the next fifteen years. There was no debate, no exchange of ideas, no encouraging of young staff; only confrontation and the belittling of others. We had a tannoy system previously used occasionally for a few whole school notices. Now it became a means of terrorising two thousand girls and a hundred and thirty teachers as she boomed through it into every classroom whenever she wanted anyone or was annoyed about something. The voice was always angry and always about a hundred decibels. Everything stopped. Even when she finished bellowing there was a sort of stricken silence everywhere while we drew breath and tried to remember what we'd been doing. The fear that you might be next to be summoned so humiliatingly to her office forged links of sympathy and alliance between teachers who'd previously barely spoken.

Tales began to spread of unfair confidential reports given to other schools whence fleeing staff were applying. History was made a choice not a compulsory subject for half of Year Four, without discussion or prior warning. A dazed Head of Latin confessed that her subject was to be abolished altogether from September and no-one had told her if she had a job anymore or not. A Head of Home Economics didn't know whether to laugh or cry at the weeks of persecution she endured over the writing off of six broken irons. A Head of Personal and Social Education suddenly found she was Head of Careers as well without consultation, training, extra time or extra money. Letters from the Education Department to the Staff never reached us till long after any action date. The very occasional Staff Meeting was a monologue by the Head in which she listed personal successes with a few individual girls and all serious matters were studiously ignored. Control of the Chair, no Agenda, no A.O.B. and keep on talking from four o'clock till six o'clock when everyone with a family waiting at home, was so desperate to get out, meant that we were just anxious to see the back of her.

There were many cases which involved Union support so both ILEA officials and Hamilton House personnel became well known to us. The Union obviously thought one particular incident worth following up. A teacher had been suspended: accused of being Racist. It took nearly a year before the "Hearing" before the Governors so the teacher was on full pay all this time. Goodness knows what negotiations went on behind the scenes but the Head was sure she was right so no compromise was possible. It developed into a full trial with witnesses for the teacher and for the Head. Over thirty came to support the teacher but only three or four the Head.

Although the teacher was completely cleared, the resultant breakdown in relationships made it sensible for her to move to another school. At last the Governors, an unknown and distant group of people, became aware of major management problems and things must have been said which were to cause a few changes. Cosmetic changes only, like more meetings and the Head visiting the staffroom for ten minutes each lunch time. This was not popular - if for no better reason than someone had to give up a chair to her. As teachers, but not Heads, stand most of the day, this was quite a hardship.

The years dragged on though the weeks fled by. I'd become the first Teacher Governor and Chair of the Staff Association. The Head banned the Association but we met anyway. The years of dominance, self-righteousness and self-advertised leadership had made marks on us all. Those who didn't need to work left and those of us still there were discouraged and devalued. She eroded our confidence in everyway. Any meeting, whether general or private, was a confrontation to be dreaded. This loss of confidence spilled over into our dealings with the children with dire results. Not only did you know you'd have no backing from the Head in trouble, but the girls knew it too. Their confidence grew as ours declined. Discipline degenerated and there were more and more girls nobody could do anything with. There was less and less job satisfaction.

For all her vaunted leadership, I cannot think of one educational idea the Head produced. She had of course, taught me a tremendous amount about what a Head should not do. I learned how important it was to consult, support staff over discipline, encourage more modern teaching methods, avoid large groups of discontented girls and give the less able, as well as the clever, a sense of dignity and self-worth by mixing them in with brighter ones. If the staff aren't happy the pupils suffer.

I also learned never to claim, or even to think that God was on my side. The Head's remark in Assembly "God will always look after you and help you and I am in my office" was never ever forgotten.

There was lots of fun, however, and in any large school there's always so much going on that you always get a good laugh at this remark or that situation. Sometimes we gave staff entertainments to the girls, that is before we became exhausted with controversy, and I'm sure we enjoyed them more than the girls did. The whole Maths Department became the Magic Roundabout and I acquired a far deeper understanding of my colleagues as well as Dougal, Florence, Brian and Zebedee. I was Catherine Parr and learned a survival technique which was to stand me in good stead . . . speak dismissively to kings and carry on knitting. The Noel Coward play that we did was only spoiled by the Head's over enthusiastic speech of thanks at the end of the first night. As she planned to come to every performance, so we planned to take one curtain call only, then run like the wind to the dressing rooms. This we did and the curtain-puller was obliged after the third command to raise the curtain on an empty stage. The shrieks and roars from the Head, who refused to go until we'd all returned, did oblige us to return to face an audience as embarrassed as we were. She then ordered me to take off my wig to show everyone what I really looked like. I looked, I imagine, like thunder.

This was the only school I have worked in that had a full-time nurse. At least we called her Nurse though she might only have had a First Aid qualification. There was also a sick room which could hold four or five girls (it was often used for other activities) and this was most unusual. Schools do not come under factory or workshop legislation and it has always been a major problem to know what to do with sick or injured people. How ill you had to be actually to gain admission to this room I never found out. Everyone I sent over was always sent back, even the twelve year-old whose mother had died the night before and who was in considerable distress. Certainly no staff ever got in to lie down for the odd half-hour when feeling ill. You just had to be ill in public. Actually as a teacher you just couldn't afford the time to be ill. Sadly, illness often led to irritability or apathy in the classroom so a term's goodwill could be lost. Often we were all so busy and tired that we barely noticed colleagues' strain, yet people in that staffroom suffered major tragedies: unwanted pregnancies, abortion, divorce, suicide, missing relatives, burglary and bereavement. My own family problems loomed large and there were whole weeks and months when I left an unhappy home in the morning to go to an unhappy school for the day.

And we were so badly paid.

There was still a sense of vocation however and in those days you never knew what allowances other people got. I still belonged to the generation that never talked about money and wouldn't dream of asking. for more. I was now in my mid-thirties but had no car and could not have afforded the down payment on any reasonable flat. Teachers today think they are ill-paid but they seem to have a few more of the material things of life. Things were so tough that the N.U.T. organised a series of half-day strikes. In school all sorts of things were said to try to prevent staff going out and we were made to feel that we were letting all the children down. The Head (on three times my salary) vowed that she would always provide a haven for the children and implied that we were exploiters and irresponsible. Supporters of both views competed for the moral highground. Some teachers did stay but most of us departed to support the strike. The Authority had more common sense than the Head as no deduction was ever made from our salaries.

The battle over dinner duties was fought and won during this time. There still hasn't been a satisfactory solution to the problem of supervision of children during the midday break twenty-five years later. The public just presume that teachers love other peoples' children so much that they will give up half their lunch-hour to take care of them. Some Authorities make a token payment but still rely on the goodwill of the Staff. At least in the late Sixties dinner duties became voluntary.

The whole period was one fraught with strikes, anger and confrontation. My subject was challenged at every turn, the government was encouraging the movement against selection of pupils at eleven but the Grammar school lobby fought back hard. Black Papers appeared denigrating Comprehensives, Rising Hill School was closed amidst massive publicity, the school leaving age was raised to sixteen, a new public exam called C.S.E. was started with all the upheaval that goes into any new syllabus for the two final years of compulsory schooling and we were devising courses for girls who did not want to sit any exams. There were times I faced blind panic at the workload to be got through and as more and more staff left the unhappy school, so one spent more and more time showing candidates round and helping the new person settle into this enormous institution. They were nearly all probationary teachers who not only needed lots of help but who were often ill as, like most new teachers, they picked up every infection going round.

Teachers really are expected to be ill in the holidays. Until the Eighties their classes had to be taken by other staff unless it was a long term illness, and a busy person often found that a crucial piece of marking or phoning had to be dropped to take someone's class. Even in the Eighties teachers have to cover for the first three days and that may well mean that twenty-five teachers have to forego marking time.

I had now reached a crisis point in my career. I was appalled at the thought of carrying on teaching for the rest of my life. I was bored with the teaching, fed up with the lack of proper management, disappointed at the calibre of new staff and exhausted with controversy. My private life was on a slightly more even keel so I began to look around for Deputy Headships. I had had seven-and-a-half years of running tremendously hard to stay in the same place, yet I had learned more about the profession in those unhappy years than in the nine previous happy ones.

CHAPTER EIGHT

KEYS AND GRAFFITI

For over a year I had regularly glimpsed the horror of being stuck in a job I had grown to hate. Yet another year began in the September and I faced more confrontations, non-stop marking, growing disorder in classes, a nearly new department and the loss of many friends on the staff who had been lucky enough to get posts elsewhere. The classes themselves were not too bad once I was actually in them, but to look ahead was to look into a pit of horror. I had been teaching now for over sixteen years and there was little satisfaction in the classroom. One sea of faces replaced another and I was too tired and bored to keep on trying to become fond of individuals. The exception was the Sixth Form who were always a pleasure except that I was tired of teaching the Nineteenth Century. I started to apply for deputy Head posts. This was not just because I was stale and unhappy but I found I now had strong views on whole school matters such as discipline, managing people, in-service training and the curriculum.

Once you started on the interview circuit you met the same people many times. They all seemed confident and forceful. The procedure was always the same: a look round the school in the morning and a chance to ask questions from a small group of selected senior staff, then the interviews in the early evening. The whole process was over in a day and you only had about forty minutes to impress the Governors that you were the right person for the job. Usually all the Governors turned up for a senior appointment and it was intimidating to go into a strange room and face about twenty strangers chaired by another stranger who might or might not be a good chairperson.

The interview for Battersea County school was much as usual but I was unnerved when the chairman went round the table asking each Governor in turn whether he or she had a question. About three-quarters had no question. One asked me what I was reading at the moment and another what hobbies I had. In no time at all we were right round the table and I thought I was going to be out in under five minutes; not only rejected but rejected in record time. However, there were still the Head himself and the Inspector to ask me something and the interview proceeded for the appropriate forty minutes. There was no training whatsoever for Governors in those days and many of them were very embarrassed at not having the faintest idea what to ask. You could get outrageous or impertinent questions from some people and silence was no bad thing, unless of course, it reduced your self-confidence by implying you were a total bore.

Once everyone has been interviewed, a process lasting perhaps three hours, the interviewees settle down to an uneasy period of waiting. The false camaraderie dies away as each one wonders how the debate is going among the Governors. Some boards were quite quick and summoned the successful candidate back in half-an-hour, others took longer and you sat uneasily for nearly an hour. This board took three hours. By the time I was summoned and offered the post I was too tired to rejoice. Not too tired to accept it however, despite my reservations about what I had seen during the morning visit. I was escaping from an unhappy situation and I had to pray I was not going from the frying pan into the fire.

The Christmas holiday passed in total terror. What had I done? Any new job is intimidating but I was combining a lot of new elements: whole school responsibility instead of just departmental, a mixed school and more importantly a mixed staff for the first time, an inner city school where every door was locked when no teacher was present, graffiti everywhere and a London rush-hour car journey. I'd had a copy of the timetable which I'd tried to understand not knowing that it was incomplete, but in those days there was no other literature from a school and you just picked everything up as you went along. This wasn't as bad as it sounds as schools have more in common than outsiders realise and although I only knew a few Staff names, they were the names of senior staff. My last school somehow didn't seem quite so bad after all.

The day came and off I went. Who was it who said that things are never as bad as you expect? This day was far worse. The Head was away sick. In the previous ten years he'd never had a day's absence so this was his first. I found myself responsible for this whole community of nearly fifteen hundred people. In fact the Senior Master and Mistress were there to support and run everything and in any case, after the first couple of minutes, I didn't have time to consider anything but the people who rang up or came to see me.

I gained a little confidence when another headmaster rang up and I was able to answer his query about Battersea's timetable but I spent an anxious half-hour after the police rang to tell me they were bringing in six fifteen year-old truanters who'd been making themselves a nuisance somewhere. I went down to meet the police van and watched as six burly boys piled out. I had about one minute to impress both police and boys and of course I was a total stranger to both. I must have done alright as the word went round the Staffroom that it was worth sending regular pests to me to see if I could do anything with them. The very next day a teacher came to see me to ask for my help. I was flattered and promised all sorts of assistance. This foreign gentleman was about six feet three inches and of a powerful build and he confessed that a group of his pupils who'd given him trouble all last term had held him up at knife point the previous evening on the way home from school. He needed me to sort things out for him. He convinced me that he was in fear, if not of his life, of a nasty wounding. I was appalled on his behalf and promised to see the boys next day and we spent some time discussing a safe route home. That evening wasn't too happy for me as I tried to think what I could say and do with these monsters. Violence like this was something quite outside my experience.

The next day I sent for the boys. I made them wait outside my door while I sent up a last anguished prayer and then they trooped in. Five little boys aged about twelve appeared. The ground was cut from underneath my feet as I had to re-adjust everything I'd thought of saying. Of course I read the riot act and told them of the accusation and said how disappointed and appalled I'd been and how I wondered what sort of school I'd come to and all the usual things you would expect. They in their turn looked suitably amazed and horrified that such accusations should be made against them. They maintained that they'd had a conversation with this particular teacher on the way home and, trying to be pleasant and start the term on a better footing than they'd finished the last, they had shown him a piece of metal that was to form the basis of their metalwork homework. They couldn't understand how anyone could confuse this with a knife. In the dignified tones of the misunderstood, they assured me they would never have anymore conversations with this teacher outside class or brandish pieces of metal etc. etc. etc.

I was almost in a worse situation than before as I now had to see the teacher again and tell him that, though I believed his story, I couldn't accept that twelve year-olds like these constituted a serious threat, and that if he couldn't control little boys like this he really shouldn't be teaching. I was a great disappointment to him and I think he really was afraid, but there was no question of going to the police or doing more than writing home. He left at the end of term.

Later on I was to have to deal with a range of things and there were certainly a few pupils who were beyond control. The recalcitrant boys tended just to stay away but the girls kept coming, presumably to meet their friends, so often were a more serious problem. Two boys who had decided that education was a waste of time lived in a nearby high-rise flat with a woman who was unknown to us, though certainly not a relative. They sometimes visited the playground in the lunch time and on one occasion took two girls back with them and raped them. This of course became a police matter as my part in the affair was little more than finding that the girls were missing from afternoon school, listening to a selection of garbled and contradictory stories from classmates and then calling the police. It was a Friday afternoon so I spent a ghastly weekend wondering if they were alright. The girls reappeared on Monday seemingly subdued but not traumatised, and I learned that the police were bringing charges against both boys. A year later I was asked to take one of them back in school as he hadn't reached the school leaving age of sixteen, but I refused. He may well have been a reformed character but the girls were still at school and I didn't think they should have to put up with him and the resurgence of gossip.

As far as I know we had few fights in school. The policy was simple. Both pupils were excluded for a period. Even an innocent victim would have to be at home for a day to let matters cool down and guilty people were out for longer. There was a sort of sliding scale of exclusion and the interesting thing was that even those who disliked school didn't like being excluded. It wasn't just that it went on their record but it was a personal rejection. Nobody likes to think they are totally unwanted.

We did occasionally have fights outside after school, both between individual boys and boys from other schools. There was usually a strange atmosphere during the afternoon and we could sense the anticipation, then people left school at the final bell but just hung around outside. Great crowds of four or five hundred milled around and staff all rushed out to try to disperse them. The interesting thing was that we could and did move them on and we never had a fight in sight of the school. Very few of them did actually develop into fights at all and those that did, took place without a great audience and well away from authority.

Half the trouble, in fact, more than half the trouble, came from the supporters and hangers-on who stirred matters and, made it impossible for boys to withdraw. Girls were very much to blame in this respect.

I mentioned that all doors at Battersea were locked whenever there was no teacher present. This led to appalling congestion in the corridors before every lesson. On the bottom corridor, which was mainly the Maths corridor, you could have one hundred and fifty people all crammed into a tiny area. The teacher had to fight his or her way to get through to open the door. Yet everyone remained remarkably good humoured. Each door was covered with graffiti yet no-one could have got a hand up to write or carve anything, so great was the crush. The graffiti must have been done by a leisured pupil temporarily sent out from the class. The doors were all locked because we had some light-fingered pupils who would steal anything moveable, and a few things that weren't. Scissors, globes, feltpens, paper, typewriters, tools and even sewing machines disappeared like magic and many a lesson ended with bags being searched. This was very much resented by everyone, including the teacher who had to do it. No item ever turned up in a bag but if the teacher really meant business it reappeared behind a radiator. Of course, something heavy like a sewing machine needed planning, an escape route and transport later in the day, but that was certainly within the competence of a skilled operator. For days the staff tried to work out how Mike, aged thirteen, had managed to get two stereo speakers down from their reinforced connections twelve feet up on a wall in a locked classroom. He'd only had about five minutes unaccounted for. We never did find out, but we found the speakers hidden behind a bush in a tiny garden that hardly anyone remembered was there. We could never prove it was him but he took no exception to the grilling he got and when the whole school gave him the credit for a lightning piece of work he assumed a modest smile and issued no denials.

Very few pupils stole of course, but you just need one thief in any community to create misery, distrust and hours of investigative work. Yet the thieves and the criminals were often so charming. I had to learn to put aside my puritanical, rather self-righteous attitude to wrong doing and be much more relaxed about it or I didn't get any response at all from anyone. This was the specially good thing about the Head and the Staff at Battersea. They could and did act against these offences but they never lost their liking for the pupils themselves. This liking shone through the whole school, stemming from the Head, and most youngsters knew they were respected for themselves. As a consequence, we had no major discipline problems of control, few ugly confrontations, no gangs intimidating people, and I was unaware of much colour problem. The atmosphere was cheerful and laid back.

The Heads of House worked very hard with their pupils and a tremendous amount of social work was done, either directly or through Social Services. Some youngsters were desperately poor and probably relied on our excellent school dinners for survival. Others were left alone in flats and houses while relatives went abroad for long periods. One had a father so regularly drunken that when ever the family managed to get a piece of furniture it finished up in fragments on the pavement, whence it had been hurled. To create the atmosphere which enabled youngsters to confess these things was no small achievement, as I learned how very, very loyal they were to their ghastly families. Nearly all of them were growing up with an amazing amount of dignity and a clear knowledge of right and wrong. It was at this school, which had the most social deprivation of any I had worked in, that I really learned to have confidence in the future generation. They were kindly, generous, unambitious and eminently sensible.

Of course we were let down by a few. Peregrine had a high sounding name and a charm of manner that had got him his House master's second best overcoat and other help to outfit him to quite a high standard. When he was arrested for mugging an elderly lady we didn't believe it and it wasn't until he asked for eighty-nine other offences to be taken into consideration, that we had to accept that this smiling lad was pretty rotten. He came back to school slightly abashed but he couldn't charm us as before and soon removed himself permanently.

There were laws about school attendance but they seemed unenforceable and I spent many hours trying to get pupils or their parents taken to court. I can only remember one case coming up and the parent was ordered to send the boy to school. He came the next day but never again. The law was a laughing stock. Just like those boys, and they were nearly all boys, who were arrested for some offence but were given probation which they said quite openly was "getting off".

There was a clear distinction between home life with its leisure and the school. All those from ordinary homes confided in friends but not teachers. They had no need of us. In the early seventies however, the sexual laxity of the Sixties had certainly affected young teenagers at schools. This seemed a problem particularly for the girls. By the time a girl was fourteen or fifteen the pressure was on not only to have a boyfriend but to have sex with him. Most of them were far too young and many were pressurised to have an affair with someone they didn't really care for. As they all read magazines which emphasised the importance of true love they had to cope at their age with the disappointment of the act itself and their failure to have an intense and permanent relationship. This was something that most of them could not talk about and you would find weeping girls in odd corners who wouldn't talk to anyone. Some took to the life with abandon though and the school was often a hotbed of gossip. We even had a period when experienced girls boasted by wearing thick black knee socks and were openly contemptuous of those wearing the more normal tights or socks. This eventually passed, much to our relief, as we felt unable to comment publicly, despite our unease about the pressures that were brought on nearly everyone.

How people dressed became a constant topic of debate. There was a navy blue uniform which was simple and quite smart. Eleven year-olds appeared proudly in it each September, but as time went on, they became first casual then slapdash and eventually uncaring about their appearance at school. Some didn't get replacements as they grew out of things so wore something they did have which gave others the excuse to say at home that the uniform didn't matter. Once a parent had spent money on a non-uniform pair of trousers they were most unwilling to buy a uniform pair. We were glad to see truanters back whatever they wore. By the time youngsters were sixteen they had no intention of spending their hard earned money on uniform. Meanwhile some teachers were getting more and more fed up at having to enforce the rule. They hated starting each day with telling people off and the effective ones objected when other tutors let offenders slip by. Pupils who wanted to avoid a confrontation just came in late. Probably on this matter there was no strong lead from the Head.

Eventually, after long discussion, we said that uniform need no longer be worn in Years Four and Five. It had never been worn in the Sixth, who were very smart in the nearest they could get to a suit. The results of this were appalling. The problems we'd had with the senior pupils, we now had with Third Years who anticipated their elevation to the Fourths. The Fourths and Fifths came in splendid clothes for a week or two until they realised that school life took quite a toll on light blouses or too tight trousers. Everyone became very competitive and pupils from families which refused to pay large sums to show their status, felt humiliated. I have actually heard a girl say she knew her father thought a lot of her because he paid nineteen pounds for a pair of shoes for her. I had never had a pair of shoes which cost so much, but I was old enough to withstand such emotional blackmail. Younger people would find it harder.

Some people came in totally unsuitable garments and we had to try to explain that some things were only suitable for the beach and that people must be modestly dressed. Worst of all, some people decided that either they didn't care what they wore or that they weren't able to compete so they just wore the same thing day in and day out. Of course people had done this with their uniform but uniform is designed to do this and the fabrics are chosen so that they will wash well. Not so these silks and tight synthetics. Six months after abolishing the uniform we realized what a collection of absolute sights we had. Nobody cared what they wore to school and quite a few never bothered even to wash their clothes. I don't know whether it's true that uniform gives a corporate identity; I do know our decision was a mistake.

Lots of personalities remain in my mind from Battersea yet any school has a majority of pleasant, unobtrusive youngsters who go about their affairs, doing their best at lessons and learning to cope with the fifteen or so adults each year who make constant and surprising demands on them. They never seem surprised at teachers' histrionics, their irritability or their weird choice of subject matter and they even listen tolerantly to sermons on the need to be ambitious or have Higher Education or save money. Ideas which were not valued in all homes. One bright pupil remarked, "We don't have careers Miss, we have jobs".

Battersea was the first school I had been in which tackled seriously the problem of motivating the large numbers of fourteen to fifteen year-old pupils who had had enough of the watered down Grammar school courses which was all that was on offer in the majority of schools. Since we wanted our pupils to have every opportunity, we were tied to the examination system so that they could get qualifications. Many benefited and went on to the sort of jobs or training that teachers approve of but there were families, and hence pupils, who couldn't have cared less. This was a learning experience for me too. However, we were stuck with each other for the two final years of compulsory attendance and it was up to the school to interest and do our best for the youngsters.

We did it by giving them very considerable and genuine choice. Everyone had to do Maths and English but after that they could choose their five other subjects. We weren't able, nor would it have been appropriate, to allow weird combinations or tiny classes or too early specialism, but it was certainly possible to avoid subjects you'd grown to hate or in which you considered yourself a failure. Not only was there genuine choice but there was a lot of consultation with both the pupil and the parents; a process which took several months to complete. This became standard policy all over the country in the Eighties but Battersea was a pioneer. It was a successful motivater, not a shadow of a doubt, but it brought with it a serious problem which we failed to address.

What we couldn't do, and on reflection didn't even try to do, was to run two examination courses in each subject; G.C.E. as well as C.S.E. Both staffing and accommodation were insufficient to do that throughout but we could have done it in a few subjects. There were not many pupils who could have passed G.C.E. at sixteen but the few there were had to stay another year and enter in the Sixth. The laid back attitude which gave the school excellent staff-pupil relationships also meant a casual attitude to homework and the discipline of study. We responded by accepting a lower academic standard from the twenty or thirty (out of nearly two hundred and forty) who might have been pressurised into aiming for G.C.E.

How serious a failure was it I wonder?

The attempt to motivate youngsters went side by side with effort to give them some cultural background. As well as seven exam subjects, everyone had to do twelve week non-exam courses in things like Art, Drama, Sociology, Home Handyman, Television criticism, Careers, Typing etc. Setting this up was something I enjoyed very much; not just the time tabling but the negotiation with the Department Heads, each of whom was expected to contribute something worthwhile to this complicated rotation scheme.

What I didn't enjoy much was taking Assembly. The Head was an agnostic and had instituted the custom of just talking to half the school once a week: Mondays for Seniors, Wednesdays for younger pupils. I remember talks on Pablo Cassals, the importance of thinking of others, the current famine or war, this or that famous person, problems facing the sick or elderly and on a range of simplified articles clipped from his Sunday newspaper. They were usually short and worth listening to, but said little to the spiritual side of our nature. We then had a short prayer and it was on to the notices.

The tone in the Staffroom was very anti-Assembly, indeed anti-religious and every so often edicts would go out to teachers to try to force them to stay in Assembly with their tutor groups. Not only did the mass departure of every member of staff give its own message to the school, but the Head and I were left to cope alone with perhaps seven hundred lively youngsters. Teachers do have the right to absent themselves on religious grounds, yet in nearly forty years of teaching I have only known about four people who have actually come and said that they declined to go into Assembly.

Thinking of things to say in Assemblies is a constant nightmare. Whatever you do is wrong according to many people and boring according to the rest. Let one scrap of personal conviction creep in and you are accused of brainwashing innocent children; while any mention of Jesus Christ brings down the whole multi-cultural lobby on your back. Inviting others in to speak is a disaster more often than not, as inexperienced people can neither assess the ability level, the attention span, nor what actually interests those particular young people. You really have to be quite good to hold the attention of several hundred pupils of varying ages.

I spent the whole week planning what I would say when it was my turn and I always tried to have some sort of a story. One teacher was perhaps more accurate than she thought when, with a slight slip of the tongue, she said loudly in my hearing, "I'm sick of these stories with silly morals". Though she agreed when I asked if she really meant silly stories and not silly morals, I'm not sure whether we hadn't reduced Assembly to a point where she was right the first time.

Few families went to church yet the vast majority of youngsters would tell you that they did believe in some Superior Being. This affected their lives only in so far as they thought it important to be kind to people. This is the faith of children and is lovely for ten year-olds, but how can the spiritual side of one's nature be developed if any talk of such matters is discouraged. Sixteen year-olds would not be allowed to get away with such naive statements about politics or literature or history. Perhaps that is the answer. Learn and question the deeper values through those very subjects. Yet I wonder what positive spirituality can be learned from studies of Macbeth, Prospero, Lord of the Flies, The Irish question, the causes of World War One and the Trade Union movement. Lots of values and actions to disapprove of, of course. Yet in so many ways Battersea was good in treating people positively. Tolerance was valued along with generosity, community spirit and a love of life. I'm not sure about selflessness, gentleness or coping with pain and failure. Certainly nothing at all about prayer and no guidance about where to find teaching on these matters.

I do feel that schools play a vital role in this sphere of adolescents' growing maturity yet Society itself sends contradictory messages to teachers. One minute you've got the government saying that the Christian religion and values must be taught, another you're told that a multi-cultural approach is essential, then again any personal statement of faith is interpreted as undue pressure while a large section of your audience feels such matters are totally irrelevant. The vast majority of the population never goes near a church except for weddings and funerals, yet the school is by law required to take an act of worship every day. EVERY DAY!

Among the great pleasures of being a senior member of staff are front seats at school concerts and plays, seeing all the Art work before it was despatched to examining boards and meeting all the visitors that the Local Authority sends to look round English schools. These visitors are legion. They cause a great deal of disruption as they always want to go into classes and these classes have to be carefully chosen. Not so much from the pupils' point of view as all the pupils then felt so special, but from the point of view of suitable subject material and a teacher who felt confident in front of strangers. Then of course, no-one wanted visitors to see the mad and the bad.

One area we were proud of was the Reading department. Secondary schools normally expect pupils to be able to read fluently when they arrive at eleven. I still think that this is reasonable but at Battersea we had well over half of our intake with a reading age below their chronological age. We had about half of those, that is about sixty children, with a reading age of less than eight and-a-half. Most of them boys. This meant that they couldn't read any text book for any subject. They might have been mathematical geniuses but we would never have known as they couldn't read the problem, so couldn't even start.

Probably primary schools, parents and society must take equal blame for this sorry state of affairs. I do believe that children must be read to from an early age, by fathers as well mothers; that football stars and television heroes must be seen to be enjoying reading, and that small boys should understand that strong men love reading just as much as driving cars.

We had to pour a lot of our resources into appointing extra staff to address this problem. We could only cope with the sixty with the lowest scores and even then had major problems as there simply were no suitable books for them to read. While we congratulated ourselves on achieving considerable success, we tended to forget that another sixty in the year were also struggling with books that were too difficult. Apart from the practical problems, we had to avoid giving the poor readers a sense of failure else they would have given up entirely. We believed praise and appreciation were more likely to encourage pupils to work to overcome disadvantages.

If I ever had a moment at the beginning of the academic year I would stand in the staff corridor and wait for the lesson-change bell to ring. Then I could see one thousand, three hundred and fifty people get up from what they were doing and go to do something else. Forty minutes later they moved again: and so on; seven times a day, five days a week. Not only had I made the timetable but I had contributed to the sort of subjects on offer, I had helped to maintain an orderly community and played some part in establishing that vital but elusive element, the ethos of the school.

It had been exhilarating and rewarding but now it was time to move on.

CHAPTER NINE

TEA-POTS AND POLITICIANS

Eventually I became a Head.

Not only had I got to the top of the greasy pole but I'd got a lovely school with a good reputation and, as a surprising bonus, it was only a short drive from home. It was a true comprehensive school in that there was an enormous ability spread in each year group, ranging from very clever girls who would undoubtedly make University, to some extremely backward ones. It had been a grammar school and the Fifth Year was still a selected group but the other year groups were comprehensive both in ability and social background.

I had become totally committed to comprehensives in the Sixties after reading Robin Pedley's book. I liked teaching clever pupils but I couldn't accept the English system of testing all eleven year-olds and rejecting about seventy-five per cent of them. Make no mistake, as a result of such testing, both children and their parents considered they had failed. They tried to hide their feelings and spoke bravely about good opportunities elsewhere, but for most, wherever they went next would be second best.

A good self-image is vital for success and to damage that seriously in childhood is not only a form of abuse but cripples the future workforce of the country. Anyway, who on earth can draft an examination that foretells at eleven, potential at sixteen? If we could, every grammar school in the country would get hundred per cent grade 'A's every time, and secondary moderns never.

Too often, children accept the labels adults give them and any prophecy becomes self-fulfilling. I had been in schools where the girls in the bottom stream of an academic, selective school showed by their behaviour, attitude and work standard that they didn't expect to succeed. The D stream in each year group became a serious problem and staff exacerbated the situation by constant nagging, expressions of disappointment, threats of retribution and fears for future failure. Yet the very fact that they had been selected showed they had been clever girls at eleven.

Nobody thinks that everyone has the same amount of ability; indeed, a great range of ability is apparent both in written work, oral work and social skills from the first week. The way to cope with this is through group work, different targets, helpful comments on work instead of marks, the encouragement of questions and by giving some value to everyone's work. There are subjects like Maths and German which are linear in structure, that is, you can't understand the second lesson until you have really mastered the first, and in that case it is wrong to keep brighter children back by constantly attending to the slower ones. In those circumstances the pupils can see their own problems and are reasonably happy to work with others of a similar ability level. That is called setting (as opposed to streaming) but it makes heavier demands on resources. The majority of subjects can be taught for some years so that pupils of varying abilities respond in their own way at their own level.

So I was proud to be the Head of a Comprehensive school and proud that it was Twickenham County School.

There were some surprising bonuses. One was that I received an invitation to a concert given by the Head of Music and the pupils in Hampton Court. This was terribly grand and everyone came in long skirts and brought a picnic and wine to eat in the grounds. Just to sit in the Great Hall and listen to lovely music was thrill enough but we were also summoned back after the interval by the trumpeters from Kneller Hall. I wondered what further splendours were to be revealed about the school. Everyone had heard of Twickenham and this was an advantage; I never had to repeat the name of the school. Indeed we could see the great rugby ground from our playing fields. Whenever there was the Oxford and Cambridge University match we all went home a bit earlier to miss the traffic congestion and drunken crowds. Another benefit was a partial cure for my fear of flying. Each lunch time I walked round the school and watched the planes flying into Heathrow over the spectators' stand; one every forty seconds. Nearly fifty planes an hour and never an accident: who was I to think I was singled out for an incompetent pilot or a grotty plane? The reverse side of the coin was the noise they made during Assembly and lessons but the girls just patiently waited until the plane had passed and the lesson could continue.

This school had a uniform of dark brown and everyone wore it. Coming from the do as you please attitude of Battersea it was a welcome sight and as I myself had worn brown as a girl there was a sense of belonging straight away. If everyone is in uniform you stop noticing what people wear and look directly at their faces.

How do you prepare for your first day as a Head?
You read everything you can get from the school. You study the timetable and curriculum. You visit, perhaps twice, and meet as many staff as you can. You have a long session with the two Deputies to find out the main issues and the pattern of the days and in particular the first day. Everyone needs the security which comes from a recognisable structure; existing staff and pupils as well as the hundred and eighty new girls just as nervous as me. You also start reading the local paper and that gave me a nasty shock. Before I'd even taken up my post headlines shrieked that Twickenham School would be closed. That meant letters, meeting with worried staff, a trip to see the Director of Education and the realisation that I was now in the political arena. An arena for which I was totally unprepared. To show how naive I was, I believed the Director when he said there were no plans to close the school.

To me the most immediately important thing was to take two Assemblies. Two because the whole school could not get into the hall. A bad impression here would be pretty devastating and could take ages to eradicate. I well knew that adolescent girls could be the harshest of judges. I spent ages trying to think of sparkling, witty, inspiring stories that could somehow sum up everything I thought important, but nothing seemed good enough. Eventually, I abandoned the lot and read from the Bible the story of how Solomon had asked God for wisdom, and said I hoped people would not think me too presumptuous if I asked to be given the same. I then abandoned this humility and made them all pray for me.

I was extremely nervous whenever I took Assembly but in a strange way, when eventually I stopped being nervous I stopped having anything worth saying. They were an important way of affecting the ethos of the school; not that anyone is likely to be changed by one assembly, but over a five- year period there must be some effect. I had a favourite story which came out every year. The Emperor of Persia was delighted with the chess board given him by a skilled craftsman and offered him a reward, up to half his kingdom. The craftsman asked for one grain of rice to be put on the first square, two on the next, four on the third and so on. Each square was to have double the last. The Emperor laughed and agreed, thinking he had had a good bargain. He was no longer laughing as the rice was first counted and then weighed out. One, two, four, eight, sixteen, thirty-two, sixty-four, a hundred and twenty-eight . . . . . by square ten it was five hundred and twelve, by square sixteen it was thirty-two thousand, seven hundred and sixty-eight and that was only a quarter of the way across the board. I usually left the school to work out the total for the final sixty forth square as I myself had never got past one billion, nine hundred and eighty-nine million, eighty-three thousand, nine hundred and four at square thirty-three. It was easy then to talk about the accumulative effect of good habits and pleasant thoughts. First a thought, then an inclination, then a habit, then a way of life and lastly a destiny. I was full of encouragement and hope as I looked at the clear young faces in front of me.

Another story much beloved of Heads in assembly is Hans Anderson's The Emperor's New Clothes and I have told that often. On one occasion I praised everyone who'd identified with the fearless, truth-speaking little boy. Then I praised all the mature people who had modestly wondered if they were unable to see the truth and heard only what they wanted to hear, like the Emperor. But I finished up wondering if a few of us were actually the con-men. I knew that some of my pupils would think that if you worked hard and were kind you would get a good job, a loving family and live happily ever after. I never actually said this although I frequently implied it. However, a Head who is constantly doubting herself is no use to anyone and we do have to hope our next generation will have a positive approach to life. Cynicism at eighteen may be a necessary stage but it is unhealthy at thirteen.

Getting used to a new school is not difficult. What is difficult is getting used to a new Education Authority. Coming from the Inner London Education Authority with its enormous resources and enlightened concern both for disadvantaged youngsters and curriculum development, it was a shock to have to deal with a smaller organisation staffed, in a few cases, with resentful people who had been moved from the school or post they had had originally.

There was so little money. Although I had tremendous authority over staff and pupils the financial stringency was such that I had to get permission from my governors for every item of expenditure over seventy-five pounds. An electric typewriter needed specific permission from the Education Authority. No reprographic equipment later than 1940 was provided and a school of over nine hundred was run with less than two full-time office staff. And they were mainly term time only. We had only three telephone instruments and everyone had to ask the office for an outside line. Goodness knows why we asked for an outside line, as inside calls were never possible. Things were to improve gradually but the solution didn't finally come until we were given our own budget in the late Eighties. So I started with an annual budget of about five thousand pounds in 1977 and finished with one of one-and-a-half million in 1990. The school did far better out of the second, despite initial fears of staffing costs and I no longer had to grovel to clerks who had no particular interest in our school for redecorations or repairs. I could grovel away for extra staff but I never got more than the quota, and it was a less generous quota than ILEA'S.

You do eventually learn who to contact for what, how to keep out of the way of a flamboyant Director who talked of education for the next millennium, who your friends are among the other Heads and which Inspectors were just filling in time. I managed to get the paint work changed from the darkest brown imaginable to white and get classrooms out of the Victorian period. Just how difficult it could be to get a large external body to do something for your school is illustrated by the hours I spent trying to get workmen to put up pin boarding. It seemed to be so simple that it never got done. But I wanted children's' work on the walls, for decorative as well as social reasons, so an amazing amount of time as well as a proportion of our tiny budget went on this.

Principles of economy were so well instilled that the teacher in charge of stationary for the whole school doled out microscopic amounts of paper. Staff were constantly irritated by her parsimonious attitude and her refusal to open the cupboard except very briefly on Fridays. Trying to introduce some Computer Studies meant a disproportionate amount of money went on our one computer and we simply hadn't the resources to do more than introduce our first years to it. The club that was started was well supported however.

Now that Heads have their own budget there is no problem about getting work done and it is nice to be wooed instead of being the wooer. It also means that the uninteresting job of ensuring proper maintenance can be delegated.

Graffiti is a problem in most schools and on arriving I had been impressed with the purity of the toilet walls in Twickenham. I don't mean that there was none but that every small scribble was obliterated immediately. One room that we failed totally with was one given to a Fifth Form in Mendip Lodge. Mendip was an old house with leaning walls, uneven floors and the colour schemes of the Thirties. The class had used felt pens (which were fairly new then) to write over every wall AND the ceiling. There were disparaging remarks about some staff and me, names of music Groups, rude words meant to shock, Heil Hitler, political slogans left over from the Sixties and other rather self-conscious phrases. The effect was appalling. So much for the trusted seniors of a school that considered itself prestigious. So much also for their Tutor who had taken no action until the ceiling was covered and who had totally failed to be aware of the mood of anger which must have motivated the graffiti. Both the teacher, the pupils and the house needed a sorting out but only the first two got it. No money, of course, to improve the ghastly working conditions.

Some of the same sixteen year-olds were involved in the only major mutiny I ever had to deal with. They had written a list of things they disliked about school life and given this to a member of the office staff who came and put it in my in-tray half-way through the afternoon. I was busy and paid no attention. On going up to the Staffroom later I was surprised to be congratulated for my cool head. Not understanding this comment I asked what the Deputy meant, only to be told that the whole of Year Five was out on the field refusing to come in to any lessons. I couldn't believe my ears. It was then about a quarter-of-an-hour before home time, so I decided that it was better to remain in ignorance and let their protest fizzle out. I shot back to my office to read the list of grievances and to prepare myself for the next day. The grievances included:

No more Assembly
No more Uniform
The right to go out at lunch time
To stop being treated like children
No compulsory R.E.
A School Parliament

All this on a scrappy bit of paper and unsigned. They hadn't the courage to give their list directly to me yet they certainly didn't lack self-confidence as they had rung up one of the London Evening papers and a short piece duly appeared.

By next day I had worked myself into a fury and gave the whole year group the benefit of my very considerable anger. It postponed for some time the plans I had already formed for starting a School Council, but later in the year I did allow them to leave school at lunch time if their parents agreed. It turned out to be a mistake but at least when I rescinded this the next year, the rest of the school could see why.

The rest of the school was happy, well disciplined and hard working. The time flew by, measured not by months but by the annual landmarks in school life: exams, report writing, new First Years, Harvest Festivals, Easter Bonnets, Christmas Post-boxes, concerts, sponsored walks, Borough Sports, mufti days, Book Searches, Christmas dinners, Carol concerts in St. Mary's Church, termly Governors' Meetings, bad behaviour from a few after breaking up and the Oxford and Cambridge Boat Race.

This event was a relic dating from the time the race was of overwhelming interest to the whole riverside community. The local interest had gone but the school tradition of a race between the prefects and the staff lived on. All new staff were forced to take part and, once my own turn was over, I enjoyed watching. Both sides dressed up and competed to extort money from the watching school, to line the banks of the river chalked in blue across the playground. We all enjoyed the sight and screamed encouragement for gangsters with violin case collecting boxes or dustbin liner dressed teachers or masked mice or flappers or whatever. A lot of money was collected for charity and a good time had by all.

The girls chose the charity. I had set up a School Council once the girls, who had been striking on the field had left, and they made the decision. There were many other charities as each form collected each week. Over the year a lot of money was sent off to worthy causes and it still makes me angry when older people talk about the selfishness of youngsters. I have never known children fail to respond to any tragedy in whatever way they can and usually they are more sympathetic than their critics.

A regular highlight was the Christmas entertainment. Some

times the staff gave it, sometimes the Fifths. The assistant caretaker was regularly called on to play Father Christmas or J.R. Ewing or Prince Charles while all the men on the staff could be assured of starring roles. Once I was summoned from my front seat to be a tea-pot and the sight of me with one arm a handle and the other a spout was enough to send everyone hysterical. The words of wit were often drowned by the cheering and laughter but they did much to raise spirits and humanise relationships.

Girls became less confrontational as they enjoyed themselves and realised they were trusted. One small thing got rid of an enormous amount of unconscious resentment. We opened the school doors early in the morning. This was a relief to those who came early or a long distance and it showed that we trusted them. No longer did they have to wait outside until eight thirty-five. The only ones to object were the cleaners, but the girls just sat around chatting so caused no problem. No classroom doors were locked and classes could go into a room without waiting for the teacher. This could only last as long as there was good behaviour, but coming from the fortress security of Battersea it was a relief.

It all continued to be a learning process for me too but I felt strongly that the whole emphasis of the school was on academic work. I didn't want these standards to be eroded but I had learned at previous schools that people must be seen to be valued for what they are as well as what they can do. I didn't know, or even want to know, nine hundred names but every girl must be well-known to several people and one of them must have authority to bring in parents or social services as necessary. The old system that channelled all this through one person was totally inadequate.

Nowadays, we are all familiar with systems of pastoral care but they were still being debated in the Seventies. No staff objected to the system of Houses I set up, after discussion, but they didn't feel that the Heads of House should have extra non-teaching time nor that they should be paid allowances. Some Heads of Department did feel they coped adequately with pupils who had behaviour or work problems and failed to see the need. However, once the system was up and running the objections died away and now no-one knows how we ever managed without it. Pastoral staff cannot solve problems but they can help children articulate them and acknowledge that they exist. Those who can cope alone are left alone but most girls came to know that there was a sympathetic ear.

Confidences came fairly quickly. In a few years we had every imaginable problem; runaways, living rough, accusations of sexual and physical abuse, drunken parents, foreign girls left alone for weeks on end, drugs among girls in care, rape, pregnancy, arrests, (usually for shoplifting), and occasionally a drunk girl. And these were just the ones we knew about.

Staff were appalled at some of the things revealed. Ninety per cent of the girls had no problems whatsoever but the other ten did. They were often the girls who took up a lot of staff time as they had behaviour problems. Behind the charming, middle-class facade, some pretty nasty things went on. One girl caused us some disquiet as she reported that her father beat her. She was a strange girl who muttered behind your back for the amusement of her friends but who never said anything directly to the teacher. She had no bruising or other signs and there was some doubt about her truthfulness, but I had learned not to ignore what girls said. As I couldn't get Social Services on the phone I rang the N.S.P.C.C. and asked them to investigate. These things always surface late on Friday afternoons yet I couldn't just go home and do nothing. The father was an academic and the family well-spoken and prosperous. The N.S.P.C.C. believed the father and obviously thought we were a group of over excited middle-aged ladies but we did report it to the Social Services on the Monday, who considered there was cause for concern and monitored matters for a long time. We were never told what they thought the problem was but that didn't matter. It was none of our business.

What was just as difficult to deal with was the pupil who never came to school at all or the one who never spoke to adults. I used to worry about the Twilight Children who went through lesson after lesson and year after year never putting their hands up and rarely having anything to say, in even a small discussion group. They were the ones whose names you could never quite remember. Their work was rather poor and their homework scrappy but somehow it was enough to keep out of trouble. Timid and retiring, they are a challenge to teachers. A pastoral system should pick them up and a chat with the Head of House followed by some praise for something they have done well, often gives confidence. Lots of children have problems speaking to adults but they should be able to chat away in their own age group.

The over-protective mother causes problems for both child and staff.   One mother would not let her fifteen and fourteen year-old daughters travel on the bus despite the journey being easy and undertaken daily by a crowd of classmates. Having children was too great an honour to risk anything happening to them.   As I never heard of anything happening on that route except gossip and camaraderie, I do hope the girls (who must now be thirty something) can manage to get around.   Peer group pressure must have affected them but the family moved away so I didn't witness the inevitable battle for independence.   One great disadvantage was that this Mother was always in the school, waiting to take them home or resting after bringing them; usually complaining of the traffic and her weariness. We had to be careful what we said as she always seemed to be around in corridors after school was supposedly finished for the day.

Secondary school should be a safe environment for learning to stand on your own feet and take a little distance from the family.

We thought the new Pastoral system helped the staff, who a few years earlier had all been Grammar School teachers, to value a range of qualities besides academic excellence.   Academic excellence too, of course.

It also made good tutoring important. The old way of going in and taking a register, hurrying to get rid of your form in Assembly then getting down to the real business of the day - teaching your subject, was no longer good enough. As more and more background was revealed we all learned to be alert to anger, withdrawal, mood changes and to give a sympathetic hearing if a girl had anything to tell us. It affected the teaching too. You simply cannot shout at someone for inadequate homework when you know they are doing six hours work in the evening in the family shop or trying to sober up a Mother who is too drunk every evening even to go to the toilet, never mind make a meal. Girls who are obliged to spend every free minute in the Mosque study group or Kingdom Hall are also at a great disadvantage. Another way has to be found. It sometimes can be found by discussing the matter with parents, but not always. Nor can the Social Services or the Educational Welfare always help.

I did not expect to be involved in these cases. There were far too many for one thing and anyway, the new pastoral system was supposed to deal with them. I just wanted to be kept informed about the most serious cases. I was more interested in curriculum development and staff development. There was little time for this, however, as political events took a more threatening turn.

There were two all girls schools in the Borough, one all boys and six mixed comprehensives. There was an imbalance in the mixed schools as they had too few girls. A lot of parents wanted a mixed school for their boys but single sex for their daughters. This was the basic cause of the imbalance but there was also a declining school roll over the borough. The population figures were indeed known for the next ten years, so the argument was that there was no need for so many schools. One could go altogether. The plan was that the two girls schools should merge and this became the official Education Committee policy.

This sounded reasonable on the surface. Our school was very angry however, as we were regularly over-subscribed and had a superb position in the centre from which we could serve the whole borough. Should we have to merge with the other school we would be in the western half of the borough and this would make travel difficult for families in the Eastern side. It would drastically reduce their choice and they would have less opportunity for an all girls education for their daughters. We also didn't see why the two girls schools should merge and pointed to the proximity of the other one to nearby, under-subscribed mixed schools.

These were in essence the arguments. Subsidiary ones emerged as time went on for some politicians wanted all the schools to be mixed. We were thus fighting not only for the survival of a central all girls school but for the very continuation of single education for girls. The battle was to rage well over a year. Led by a marvellous parents committee and chairman, we fought to keep Twickenham school alive. We had absolutely no allies as the other schools all saw us as a threat to them and would have been very pleased to see the ex-grammar school go. The battle over which schools should merge also got mixed up with rivalry over examination results. Richmond was the first borough to publish the examination results of sixteen year-olds but in the discussions which preceded this, every school protested vehemently, saying quite rightly that you couldn't judge examination results without bearing in mind the ability level of the pupils. Schools with a good intake would emerge with lots of good publicity which, in its turn, would attract more pupils. So, in this battle to stay as we were, our very academic reputation acted against us. The Heads who had been such a support in my first year now spent a lot of time attacking Twickenham.

The Campaign Team worked very hard. Every Councillor was written to and then visited. A constant stream of letters appeared in the press. Meetings of parents were held and each persuaded to contact their local councillor. The M.P.s were involved. The Chairman of the Education Committee and the Director came to public meetings. Other public meetings were held in packed halls by neutral groups like R.A.S.E. and the Organisation for Civil Liberties. We had posters and stickers SAVE TWICKENHAM GIRLS on all our cars and most of us sported similar badges. How much of it affected the girls I have no idea as they were working normally throughout, but they were informed of everything that went on and, always a good sign, they took home the notices of meetings. We organised a march through the Streets of Twickenham to lobby the Education Committee and were met by locked gates, a police presence and a refusal of any councillor to come out and meet us. The serious atmosphere dissolved in laughter when we realized that they were actually frightened of us.

In the middle of all this, asbestos was discovered in the school. At first I suspected a Machiavellian plot to have our building condemned. This would really have scuppered our campaign, but the area turned out to be small; just the boiler room and the Geography stock cupboard. In all the upheaval of trying to teach Geography without a single aid and having men in space suits in and out of the rooms and classes being re-routed, we had a welcome new topic of conversation. In the turning out we found some old daggers and a spear in the stock cupboard.

In a moment of light relief the Secretary and I went up to Sotheby's to get a valuation. I knew you weren't supposed to carry a weapon in public yet I was carrying an eight foot spear so, having noticed a policeman eyeing us and having recently become somewhat more sensitive to police disapproval, we were reduced to getting a taxi. The weapons turned out to have some value and eventually the school received about eighty pounds for them.

The campaign to save the school was coming to a head, we thought. The Education Committee was to vote on the issue and the public gallery was packed. A space which was made for twenty held about fifty and they had to wait in extreme discomfort till the very end of a long meeting to hear the debate. All discomfort was forgotten however when the vote went against the merger. We rejoiced. Next day there were cheers in the school and congratulations all round. We went out and spent all the recently acquired eighty pounds on food for a party and invited all those who had helped. We thought it a splendid way to deal with weapons.

Alas! we were too hasty. The decision made at the Education Committee Meeting was reversed at the full Council meeting a week or two later. The merger WAS to go ahead. We could and did appeal to the Secretary of State for Education and we went up to put our case to Baroness Young, but there wasn't much else we could do. The decision on our appeal came to the Director and he informed me just before the Christmas holiday.

Twickenham had only two terms left as a separate school.

CHAPTER TEN

TWO INTO ONE

Once the news of the Merger of the two schools was announced a stillness and depression fell over everyone at Twickenham. Some girls didn't care once they were assured that the school would carry on as long as the present pupils were there. Others were sorry and somewhat discouraged to find that they were in a school that the community didn't want to keep.

Everyone took a well-earned holiday and came back reconciled and refreshed. If we had to merge we would do it as well as possible. I didn't know whether I would be out of a job in July or pushed into the Inspectorate or Head of the new school. There was a debate in the Education Committee about whether the post should be advertised nationally or whether I should get first crack at it, the Head of Kneller School having gained a post elsewhere. As I had enormous support from Twickenham parents and had run a highly noisy campaign, the Conservative majority thought it politic to let me have an interview by myself. The Leader of the Liberals was against it but was on the selection panel.

I prepared for the interview as carefully as I could and actually took about half-an-hour off afternoon school to walk by the river before my interview at five o'clock. I can still remember the lovely day, despite it being January, the serenity of the late afternoon and the coming to terms with the fact that if they didn't like me I'd done my best and it wasn't the end of the world.

In one particular area I knew I was vulnerable. Although I had never said anything against Kneller school, I had made it clear that we didn't want to join with them. Would the Selection Committee appoint someone who had been so strongly against the Merger? Could Kneller staff or parents accept a Head so closely identified with the "other side"?

The gorgeous white and gold salon at York House was lit by a superb chandelier but all I could see were the five or six steps down which I had to negotiate in some extremely high heels. I was wearing a dusty blue, clinging woollen dress as I had read that blue was considered a friendly colour, and some unobtrusive pearls instead of my more flamboyant earrings. The ten or twelve people on the other side of the table looked incredibly grim. Once seated, I looked round, smiled and wished them "Good Evening". The icy atmosphere broke and most of them smiled back in what I suspected was relief. It hadn't occurred to me that they were at least as nervous as I was.

I can't remember the questions. Nothing that was unusual or controversial. The Liberal Leader remained silent until the Chairman asked if he wished to ask anything and then he surprised everyone, particularly the Director, by saying that now he had seen my charisma he had no problems accepting me. This eased the way for them to appoint me five or ten minutes later. I wasn't sure if it was the political clout wielded by my own parents or the initial smile I'd given, but I was now the Head of the new school.

First we needed a name.

There were eight suggestions of which two were the names of men. Stanley Rundle and Joseph Turner would have negated the whole principle of an all girls school: role models are vital whether as a title or within the community so they got short shrift. We settled on the name Waldegrave as we liked the sound of it and we were in an area where the Waldegrave family had had lots of estates. Permission was obtained from the head of the family and we not only had a name but a role model in that the first Countess of Waldegrave was a self-educated woman who became a noted political hostess and interior decorator. As the owner of Strawberry Hill, she entertained Gladstone, Disraeli, Salisbury and other politicians of the second half of the nineteenth century.

Once we had a name an urgent task was the structure of the school. All staff were very anxious about their jobs. The Local Authority had quite rightly said that girls should not have to travel between the two sites. This was fine by me but meant enormous time tabling problems as the teachers would have to commute. The first fight therefore was over how many extra teachers we should be allocated to allow for this movement. In the first year it would not be too bad as we had over seven hundred girls on the Twickenham, now called the Clifden, site but in the following three years there would be no new children whatsoever. If we were to maintain the specialist teaching which I considered essential, people would have to travel from the Fifth Cross site many times a week. This was where the future school would be complete and where all the new girls would come. We were given four extra teachers; reasonable in the first and last years but very tough in the two middle ones.

Then I planned the number and types of Senior posts. We'd been given four Deputies, the two existing ones from each side, and this was a lifesaver. The Heads of Department were listed and I included a new one; a Head of Craft, Design Technology. As the Fifth Cross site had what had once been a workshop I was determined that it should be restored and the subject included in the curriculum. The others were much as usual. The great problem was that we had two existing Heads of every subject. The Staff would have to apply for their own jobs and some of them were going to be disappointed.

People could see the writing on the wall. It wasn't just that some people would be desperately disappointed but that in four years the total staff had to be reduced from over a hundred and twenty to about sixty. This was not unfair in principle as the number of teachers depends on the number of pupils, with some weighting given to older and specially disadvantaged pupils. However, the thought that half our number would have to go within four years was heartbreaking. Perhaps in the late eighties we would have realized we were one slimming institution among many but in 1980 it seemed very harsh. It was a huge saving for the Borough and it was done with so little unpleasantness that other schools had no idea that they were cushioned by economies at Waldegrave.

It was solved without too much grief. One or two people were promoted to Senior Teacher and quite a few decided to retire. Pastoral and departmental posts were mainly separated so if the teacher didn't get one she got the other. A few people who got nothing they wanted went off to the Tertiary College or on year-long training courses. Although their salaries were safeguarded their status had been undermined. Everyone had to be interviewed and although we wanted the best person for the job a balance had to be maintained between the two contributory schools.

The curriculum was adapted to fit in CDT and classical studies in First Year but Seconds, Thirds and Fifths were left much as before. Those going from Third to Fourth were to have the same organisation on both sides, that is, being kept in mixed ability groups for registration and a few lessons but making choices of subjects otherwise and being prepared for the examination for which they were best suited in each subject. This did away with the separation at fourteen into those who would only do GCE and those who would do CSE. Lots of girls were then able to do a mixture.

There are ways of calculating how many teachers you need for the next five years depending on the number of classes and sets in each subject in each year. It is never definite if you allow choice in the Upper School as you have no idea who will choose what, so there should always be a margin for error. Nor can you tell what ability spread you are going to get in future years: the greater the spread the more sets you will need in the linear subjects. You really need more in all subjects but resources are finite.

There were other changes to come but the emphasis in the first year was on stability and a non-threatening coming together.

Once the news of the Merger was out a lot of parents wanted their daughters to change sides, from Clifden, which they thought would become neglected and second rate, to Fifth Cross, which they saw as the new centre of the community. This we could in no way allow. If we had allowed it we would have been admitting it was true and we would have had a mass exodus we couldn't have coped with. In fact, Clifden girls remained very dear to all of us who had started there and we were determined that they would be cherished for the next four years. Some parents took their daughters away altogether and we were sorry about that but we kept the loyalty of the great majority.

The new uniform was chosen, the timetable made for the fifty-two forms we now had, the new CDT workshop ready and the taxis ordered for the staff who were to commute but who had no cars. I must have spent almost as long sorting out problems about transport as I did on the curriculum. We had agreed that a teacher who commuted should be allowed some extra marking time and we hoped that this could be arranged straight after the journey. Unfortunately, there was no way this could be done regularly and we were faced in the busy two middle years with people who were timetabled with consecutive lessons on separate sites. If you have setting or option columns people become locked into not one but several teams and there is no room for manoeuvre. The rule was that every lesson had

112

to start on time but you could leave a class ten minutes before the
end to get to the other side. They had to have work set and a
teacher nearby was named as being in charge during the interval.

This would never have worked in a school with poor discipline
but we were able to trust the girls and they responded well most of
the time. There were problems about collecting work which you
wanted finished in class and enormous problems about collecting
homework but people managed as best they could. Eveyone became
used to seeing teachers running in and out of both sites. At least
those with cars were given priority in the carpark. I went to both
sites every day and was careful to be seen by as many pupils as
possible. As the work load shifted more and more to Fifth Cross, I
sometimes had nothing to do at Clifden but I still went and would
often stand at the foot of the stairs at change of lessons. Several
times I heard a girl say, "You can't get away from her. She's all
over the place".

I was concerned about how the girls at Fifth Cross would react to
me. I was after all from the other side. They had seen me about the
place a little during the term I was given to prepare for the merger
but I had deliberately not walked round as I had no authority until
the September. The Acting Head, one of the Deputies of the new
school was in charge, not me, so I was really just dealing with staff.
The staff must have worked hard on this point as I never felt any
resentment from anyone at all and for this I was grateful. Problems
I had were the result of normal bad behaviour.

The first day of the new school dawned. The new First years,
all two hundred and forty of them, came in, in their new royal blue
uniforms and we had over six hundred in navy at Fifth Cross and
seven hundred at Clifden in brown. Altogether, nearly fifteen
hundred. I took four Assemblies on that day, two on each site, and
four times I read the traditional Gospel passage. It was from
Corinthians 13:

Though I speak with the tongues of men and of angels,
And have not love
I am become as sounding brass or a tinkling cymbal.
Though I have the gift of prophecy
And understand all mysteries and all knowledge;
And though I have all faith so that I could remove
mountains

And have not love,
I am nothing.
And though I give all my goods to feed the poor
And though I give all my body to be burned,
And have not love,
It profiteth me nothing . . . .

Through the years as a Head I must have read that passage on the first day of each term eighty-four times yet I never grew tired of it and felt there were always depths I hadn't plumbed. Each girl heard it fifteen times in her school career and there have been girls who have returned years later to ask where the passage came from.

Some of us wanted a church service to dedicate the new school so many girls, teachers, parents and governors came to St. Mary's Church to sing and listen to an address, readings and music. The readings were all from Solomon's building of the Temple. Not that I wanted Waldegrave to be any sort of temple, but because they were all about the best of everything being used. There were gold basins and gold dishes and gold decoration and generous gifts and everyone helping.

The staff soon got to know each other and we had several groups of girls visiting the other site. The goodwill was splendid and people fell over themselves being co-operative. We continued to enter two teams for all sports and fortunately never had the two sides playing each other in any finals. For a year or two concerts were given at each site but from the beginning we did one large dramatic production together. The difficulty over rehearsals was solved by doing an Edwardian Music Hall with separate items rehearsed on separate sides. There was no rivalry and no jealousy that I was ever aware of.

The school was up and running so the politicians wanted their acknowledgement. This was to be at the official opening of the school. Having been a guest at another recent opening where the new Head was practically behind the stage curtain and stayed silent throughout and remembering Princess Margaret's question, "Where are all the girls?" when she opened a school, I was ready with a few ideas of my own. I insisted that there should be two girls from every form and that the Committee of the United Parents Association should be present. Some staff must also be present to keep an eye on the girls who were singing and watching and all senior staff had to be there. I said firmly that I expected to be on the platform and be invited to say something. I was allowed to introduce the choir and told to be brief.

The day was fraught. I had spent the night before stitching a bright blue brocade tablecloth as one official was very anxious that women's legs should not be visible in unsightly positions. This was duly in place but when the Parks Department brought all their potted plants it was obscured. Presumably the official had also harangued Parks so there was a mass effect all along the stage. The school had to be cleaned and all displays checked for graffiti. The first years were to have normal lessons in practically total silence in case they disturbed the ceremony but others not attending were sent home for the afternoon. Everything was timed to the minute for all the hundred and one jobs.

I was invited to attend the official lunch at York House which was being given for Baroness Young. She was the Government Minister who had said the schools must unite but had been invited to open the school in a spirit of reconciliation. Lady Young was late so the polite, stilted conversation carried on. After about half-an-hour a message came that she would be yet another half-hour. I was in despair. At the rate we were going the girls would be filing into the hall before we had sat down for lunch. I decided to ring school to postpone everything for three-quarters of an hour. I could just imagine the panic back there. People were no doubt already arriving and a late start meant the ceremony would overrun the end of afternoon school. Show lessons which had been so carefully prepared would be finished before the visitors were free to come round. What would they say if the girls had cleared up and were queuing at the door to go home.

Lady Young then did arrive and we sat down at once. I have never eaten a meal in such a rush and gobbled the very nice roast lamb and all the lovely things which had been prepared. We had barely finished when she jumped up and wanted to rush out to school. This was another embarrassment as, having delayed things, I couldn't suddenly speed things up too much. We arrived in school as girls were still filing in and we had to wait in the corridor, making yet more aimless conversation.

At last we got ourselves into the hall. There were at least a dozen people in the platform party facing a hall packed with about

500: three hundred strangers, fifty people I knew slightly and a hundred and fifty of our own girls and teachers. Who most of them were I have no idea. I have even less idea of why they should want to attend. I can remember nothing that anyone said or what I said or what we sang. The only memorable event was when I got a cheer from the girls when I rose to introduce the Choir. This I'm sure, was because I was the only one they recognised. We were all glad when it was all over.

Since we were so late the tour of the school was also conducted at great speed. Lady Young dutifully whisked round with me and it was obviously a relief to her too, to get among the eleven year-olds who were dying to show her all the rather special things they had been making or doing. The highlight was the new C.D.T. room. The corridor was blank and empty but when I threw open the door there was a hive of industry. Small girls with small head scarves beamed and smiled but carried on walking round on their affairs. Polishing and sanding and measuring and cutting were all going on. There was an audible gasp and Lady Young said delightedly that it was just like Snow White and the dwarves. I'm sure it was the only thing that whole day that both of us enjoyed.

The day was commemorated by an extremely expensive plaque screwed to the entrance porch. This was stolen later and I never could understand who on earth would want it.

The new school seemed to take over my life. There were so many meetings and so many strangers to get to know. The new governing body was a great change to the old Clifden, one which had prided itself on finishing its termly meeting in an hour. This one rejected the sherry I offered at the beginning and took itself very seriously. In the fourteen years I was a Head I had seven different Chairs of Governors and that was quite a burden as there is a close working relationship between Head and Chair. I got on with nearly all of them but then they left nearly everything to me. They only thing they insisted on was being present at all interviews for teachers with responsibility allowances. This was a very reasonable request and I valued most of their recommendations. The problem came when there were several good candidates with nothing much to chose between them. Then I relied on my intuition and gut feeling and usually I got who I wanted. Usually, not always.

There was no time to sit still. The merger might well take all our energies but there were many initiatives going on in the educational world and we were determined to be in the forefront of most of them. There was our great move to make the school aware that we lived in a multi-cultural society and every subject was expected to introduce material to broaden girls' outlook. There was the year of Women into Science and Engineering, and speakers and material to be arranged for that. There was Industry Year and a conference to be arranged for industrialists and our own staff and then joint curriculum and industrial projects to be set up. There was the new government Technical and Vocational Initiative which provided us with a modest extra teacher in return for setting up examination courses in both Modular and Design Technology and Graphical Communication. And there was our own initiative to introduce eight week modules in Fourth and Fifth Years: first aid, computing, theatre, electronics, architecture, tourism, and nutrition.

We had conferences for Primary Heads, we had exchanges to France and Germany, we had a Bank, a tuck shop, Young Musician of the Year, groups setting up small businesses, working parties for equal opportunities for women, Colleges doing surveys and then telling us the results and Careers Conferences. You see no immediate tangible results for any of these activities but soldier on in faith.

We had sponsored spells, sponsored silences, sponsored walks, runs and hops. We had technology days for girls and their parents. We had fêtes and social and educational evenings for parents. We were the first school in the Borough to computerise our office and we won a prestigious Schools Curriculum Development Award. We adopted a village in Somalia and introduced G.C.S.E. successfully, despite the lack of textbooks and the late arrival of syllabuses. We were involved in everything that was going on.

During these four crucial years we had dozens of break-ins. It was the early days of videos and no sooner did we buy one or two than they were stolen. No sooner had we replaced them after claiming through the insurance than they were stolen again. There were Mondays I absolutely dreaded going into school as, if the videos hadn't been stolen from Clifden, they'd been stolen from Fifth Cross. We got more and more sophisticated burglar alarms and became very unpopular in the neighbourhood when they accidentally went off in the night. The alarms didn't stop the burglaries, even the ones which were sensitive to a single foot being put on the floor. One burglar let himself in through the roof, hung suspended from a rope and handed the videos up through the skylight. On another occasion a great pantechnican drew up at a side gate on a Sunday morning and the thieves removed twenty sewing machines through a window. They hadn't even broken the glass, just removed the new putty and laid the huge pane tidily on the grass. One of the cleaners had seen it all going on from her house but hadn't suspected anything illegal.

The burglars took not only the machines but as many videotapes as they could find. On one occasion one hundred and eighty-five tapes were taken, each one packed with lesson material and the fruit of a year's work by the technician.

I think the thieves had inside information: the timing was too exact to be chance or even good guesswork. Not all our pupils were saints. I became expert at insurance forms and we arranged to have a pile ready printed to save time. We always had accurate records of serial numbers and dates of purchase so we always got the compensation. Two or three years later the police did catch a large gang in the Harrow area and prosecuted them successfully.

Exhausting!

As the four years drew to a close we were very anxious about the one hundred and twenty girls left on their own in Clifden. Fewer staff were needed to rush over to teach them and we had a smaller and smaller section of the building as our own. The Adult College was gradually coming in and we had been quite happy to release sections to them as we shrank. Towards the end, we asked if we could look round the parts that were no longer ours and duly took all the girls up, chattering and laughing. We came down in total silence. The decorations and furniture and equipment were so splendid that we were reduced to silence. The money that must have been spent on the refurbishment beggared belief. We returned to our shabby, crowded premises downstairs aware that we counted as nothing in the eyes of the Education Committee.

That summer the hall was used for public examinations for the last time and never was a group of girls sent in with so many good wishes and so much affection. The relationships which had developed between teachers and pupils were quite out of the ordinary. The girls were determined to go out with a bang,

however, and as soon as the exams were over they resumed the
rehearsals for their grand finale. They put on a performance of
"Grease" which was an absolute triumph. One or two mothers had
helped but mainly it was their own work and it was absolutely first
rate. Maybe the theme of the simple young girl getting the attractive
young man was not what the school stood for, but the rollicking
performances of those acting the male parts with vigour and
confidence most certainly did.

The curtain came down on a tremendous success.

In every way.

EPILOGUE

School life is regularly punctuated by bells: usually every thirty-five minutes. You then leave what you are doing, whether it's finished or not to go to your next class. This happens about a dozen times a day, counting Assemblies and Form Times. Occasionally you are glad to escape but not usually. Life in school becomes so intense that the world is the school. I remember pausing by a staircase window and being amazed to notice buses functioning and people walking around in an unhurried way outside.

The demands are so constant that holidays begin with a state of collapse.

Holidays for me meant getting away from all commitments and, if possible, escaping from other people. I wanted sunshine, beautiful things to visit and something just a bit out of the ordinary. I did not want to have to make myself pleasant to anyone; I wanted to be a parcel and listen to interesting lectures. I liked to go away at the end of any holiday in the hope that I wouldn't have nerves about my return. After all, every Sunday evening of term time was a misery as I tried to think of something worthwhile to say in Assembly and screwed up courage to the sticking point.

Eventually I became ill. There had been years of concentrated work even before the new Education Act which meant far more disruption and interminable evening meetings. There had been the illness and deaths of both my Mother and Aunt. After a major operation I had to go daily to the Royal Marsden Hospital for six weeks of radio-therapy and I was away from school for a term. I realised that the quality of my life during this period was better than when at work. I had time to talk to people and could regain some interest in them, I could enjoy my very limited mobility far more than the rushing around I did at school. I had time to be myself.

I decided to retire.

It was someone else's turn.